This book be¹

BELLS IN ENGLAND

The Treble Bell at Marston Moretaine, Bedfordshire.

BELLS

IN

ENGLAND

Tom Ingram

ILLUSTRATED
BY BARBARA JONES

DAVID & CHARLES
NEWTON ABBOT   LONDON
NORTH POMFRET (Vt)

British Library Cataloguing in Publication Data

Ingram, Tom
 Bells in England.
 1. Bells—England
 I. Title
 789'.5'0942   CC210

ISBN 0-7153-9004-X

First published in Great Britain 1954 by Frederick Muller Ltd

This edition published by David & Charles Publishers plc 1987

Printed in Great Britain
by A. Wheaton & Co, Exeter
for David & Charles Publishers plc
Brunel House   Newton Abbot   Devon

Published in the United States of America
by David & Charles Inc
North Pomfret   Vermont 05053   USA

Contents

INTRODUCTION   *page*   ix

1 BIM BOM   1

2 TAG-RAGS OF THE VILLAGE   26

3 INGENIOUS NOTED RINGERS   45

4 RINGING FOR SPECIAL OCCASIONS   74

5 THE BELL FOUNDRY   95

6 TOWERS AND SPIRES   118

7 BELLING THE CAT   126

8 BELLS FOR SKULLS AND MARKETS   143

9 DROWNED BELLS AND BELL BRANDS   163

APPENDICES
   (A) IRVING IN *THE BELLS*
                              by Robert Aickman   183

   (B) THE BELLS OF BEALINGS HOUSE
                              by Robert Aickman   188

BIBLIOGRAPHY   193

INDEX   201

v

Illustrations

THE TREBLE BELL AT MARSTON MORETAINE,
BEDFORDSHIRE   *Frontispiece*

THE PARTS OF A BELL   xi

THE INITIAL CROSS, STOP, AND LETTERS FROM
THE SOMERCOTES ALPHABET   1

RAISING A BELL   9

HARVEST MUG   25

WEATHER COCK   26

BUTTON-HOLE   44

RINGERS   45

MORE RINGERS   73

BADGERING   74

MAKING A CORE; THE MAN BEHIND IS STAMP-
ING THE INSCRIPTION INSIDE A COPE   95

COPES IN THE FOUNDRY   97

THE MEANS OF RESTORATION   118

HALBERTON CHURCH TOWER   119

GLASS BELLS   126

A BELLED CAT   142

QUARTER JACKS FROM WELLS CATHEDRAL   143

BLACK BELL SHAG, BY COURTESY OF EDWARDS,
RINGER & BIGG, BRISTOL   163

DUMB-BELLS   182

Acknowledgments

I SHOULD like to thank most gratefully Mr. Robert Aickman for writing appendices on "Irving in *The Bells*" and "The Bells of Bealings House"; Mr. A. A. Hughes and Mr. W. A. Hughes of Messrs. Mears and Stainbank for constant help both to me and to Miss Barbara Jones; Miss Jones herself for the drawings; Mr. Ernest Morris for reading the Bibliography and the Rev. J. G. M. Scott for reading the manuscript. I have also received most generous help from Miss Ray Gregorson, Mr. Michael McCrum, Mr. Jack Paice, Mr. Paul Taylor, Mr. Nigel Viney, and from the secretaries of societies and guilds, the manufacturers, the ringers, the clergymen, the vergers, the librarians, and collectors who have helped me to write this book.

Introduction

NEARLY everyone's life today is ordered or disturbed by the ringing of bells; in telephones, on trams and trains, at the front door, from the church tower, or at second-hand on the wireless; only people who endure the rigorous life of the most remote agricultural communities can have for background music the spheres, and animals lowing and blowing for food or love. Noise must be the most characteristic feature of this age.

This book is concerned with one aspect of noise: bells, and, from that main heading, the people who use them to make noise and the occasions on which they make it. The loudest and oldest bells are church bells, and as these have more incident in their history, so they take up a larger part than, say, the bicycle-bell; also, their manufacture is the zenith of bell-founding, so that this has been described, instead of the no less exciting casting of cow-bells. With a few exceptions, the scope of the book is confined to England, for with trains, clocks, and fire-engines making the same noise in Scotland, Ireland, and Wales as they do in England, the oecological divergencies are small. The Church in Wales, the Church of Scotland, and the United Free Church of Scotland ring bells; the Methodists, Congregationalists, Baptists, and Wee Frees do not; the Irish Protestants and Roman Catholics continue the tradition of their saints, and ring vigorously, but again no differently from the English. Also, change ringing, an English invention, is, with a few exceptions, confined to this country.

If any reader becomes interested in the study of the inscriptions on church bells, the best way to record them is first to clean them thoroughly with a soft wire brush—

this is bad for the patina but essential—and then squeeze plasticine into the letters or ornaments, to make a mould. When you get home make a little trough of your plasticine by surrounding it with a strip of tin, grease the inside lightly, and fill it with plaster of Paris to get a cast repro-´duction of the original. Old clothes, and a hat to keep the dust out of one's hair, are also essential.

Technical terms have been used in this book as little as possible, but those describing the parts of a bell are necessary, and as there are not many I have used them, and they are explained in the diagram of a bell on the opposite page. Some purists may object that the hemispherical bells are not bells but gongs, but everyone calls them bells, so bells they are here.

NOTE—
Columbia Market, described on pages 157–161, was demolished in 1960. One of the clock jacks was smashed during the demolition, but the remaining jacks and the bells from the tower were removed by the Greater London Council. Later the bells were stolen from the Council's store.

Fire engines, ambulances and police cars now use two-tone horns instead of bells. Fire engines, however, are still compelled to carry a bell.

This drawing shows a bell hung for ringing; a piece of it has been cut away to show the clapper, and the most important parts have been named. A Ring of bells is any number up to twelve tuned on a diatonic scale, the lightest, and the highest note in the ring is called the Treble, and the heaviest, and lowest note, the Tenor; the intermediate bells are designated by numbers from 2—11. A Sally is the worsted grip near the end of a bell rope—they circle the title page.

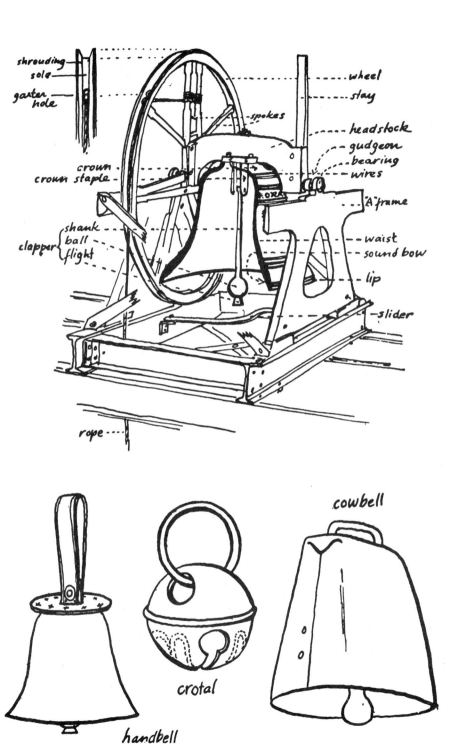

shrouding
sole
garter hole
wheel
stay
spokes
headstock
gudgeon
bearing
wires
crown
crown staple
'A' frame
shank
ball
flight
clapper
waist
sound bow
lip
slider
rope

cowbell

crotal

handbell

1

Bim Bom

ALMOST all the bells in this book are, I have said, English. The exceptions confront us at once—they are nearly all very old. For fifteen hundred years the Christian Church in this country has used bells to announce a service. When the first missionaries to these islands walked through the marshes and over the hills visiting the scattered communities in their charge, they rang small handbells to summon the people together. The bells they used were not great works of art, merely four sheets of iron bolted together, or a single piece bent into a curve and riveted down the sides, sometimes covered with brass or copper to give a less tinny tone; they were exactly like the sheep- or cow-bells which people today bring back from holidays in Switzerland or Scandinavia, and they rang with the same melancholy sound. But this was the music of the first Christian missionaries, and the reverence with which these bells were regarded attributed to them the miraculous powers of the saints themselves. None survive from England, but the Welsh, Scots, and Irish gave to these relics powers which, in their final form in the eighteenth and nineteenth centuries, before they became the property of private antiquaries or passed into museums, reflect variations of the Celtic temperament.

The Welsh believed that the sound of bells drove away evil spirits. When a corpse was being taken from the house in which it had lain to the graveyard, a small handbell was rung in front of the funeral procession; although until the custom died out early in the nineteenth century the ones used by the Welsh saints had been replaced with contemporary handbells. The only early bells which survive in Wales have been found deliberately by excavation or accidentally when draining mill-ponds or digging foundations.

The Scots have a charming story of St. Fillan's bell, which was once stolen. When the thief sat down to take a rest on his way home, he put the little bell on a stone beside him, where it stuck so firmly that it would not move till he had made up his mind to take it back. It was also a cure for lunacy; the patient was bound with ropes and dipped in a pool at Killin, and then deposited in St. Fillan's chapel for a whole night. He would be restored to his right mind if the bell was placed on his head next day. These bells had another way of inviolating themselves against theft: they rang continuously, so if the thief had tried to double-cross St. Fillan's bell it would have started to ring, protesting till it was returned. But the main use the Scots made of them was severely practical—as title deeds to property; if the hereditary custodian left the bell in his care to someone, a house or a piece of land went with it.

The Irish, with their genius for complicating life by making every act a mystery and a ritual, have more of these bells than anybody else (over sixty survive today), and they used them for taking oaths, as lie detectors, cure-alls, and excuses for sitting up all night. The oldest is the Clog Udhachta Phádraig, or the Bell of St. Patrick's Will, which was taken from his tomb in 552. About 1005 a very elaborate case was made for it, of silver and gold worked in the flat abstract patterns of Celtic art, and ornamented with Irish rock crystal. The bell itself, a shell of thin rust and iron, stays in the case, and until it was given to the Irish Academy was kept by its hereditary keepers, the family of Mulholland. No especial virtue or

2

power is attached to it other than its extreme holiness.

The Clog na Fola, or Bell of Blood, was at one time in the care of a family called O'Rorke. It is supposed to be one of the original fifty presented by St. Patrick to the churches of Connaught, and was used for administering oaths and also possessed the power of retrieving lost or stolen property. When anyone wanted to use it, he went to the O'Rorkes, paid a small fee, and took away the bell on condition that it was always held in someone's hand and that it should never touch the ground; so his family would sit round all night in a circle, each taking a turn at holding it while the rest slept. The Clog Óir was another bell which would find stolen property; every suspect would hold the bell in his hand and swear that he had not stolen. If he lied, the muscles of his face contracted so that his mouth became a horrid slit from ear to ear. So great was the reputation of this bell, that the last time it was borrowed from its owner for this purpose in the middle of the last century, the stolen money was mysteriously returned during the night before the trial. A woman in labour who took a drink from St. Mura's bell was certain not to die, and the Clog Beannuighthe, or Blessed Bell, was used to cure the sick of the Henning family of Armagh, who were its keepers. It is one of the few bells which can be dated accurately, for it is inscribed "A prayer for Cumascach, son of Ailill", who died in 904.

The Hennings would ring this bell in front of the woman wailing for the dead at the wake of a member of the family; Mr. Bell of Dungannon visited the death-bed of the wife of Paul Henning, its last keeper:

"She lay in a large badly lighted apartment, crowded with people. The bell, which had remained several days near her head, seemed to be regarded by them who were present with much interest. The vapour of the heated chamber was so condensed on the cold metal of the bell, that occasionally small streams trickled down its sides. This 'heavy sweating' of the bell, as it was termed, was regarded by every one with peculiar horror, and deemed a certain prognostication of the death of the sick woman, who departed this life a few hours after I left the room. The agonised bell, I was told, had on many previous occasions given similar tokens as proof of its sympathy on the approaching demise of its guardians."

What else could the poor bell do in such circumstances, in a hot and stuffy room full of people, but proclaim its discomfort and show that the poor woman was to die of claustrophobia and steam?

The British Museum has several of these Irish hand-bells; some stand on flat polished slabs of brown wood in glass cases in the galleries, their histories neatly inscribed in cream paint, but only their date, owner, and where they were found, no legends or Celtic mysteries. Others seldom appear and are kept in store upstairs, with more relics of the dark ages; inelegant iron slop-pails and potsherds. The bells made of iron have all been partly destroyed by rust, like the bell of Conall Cael made in the seventh century which belonged to an abbot of the church of Inishkeel. One side has been almost completely eaten away, and the only part to withstand time is a piece of bronze, decorated with Celtic curlicues, set near the top on one side.

The Bearnán Cuileáin is another iron bell; it belonged to St. Culan, brother of Cormal, King of Cashel, who died in 908. This bell is enclosed in a twelfth-century shrine very like the iron cage protecting a carboy, and made of bronze decorated with inlaid silver. Unlike St. Patrick's bell, which is completely hidden by its shrine, St. Culan's can be seen through the shrine, which only protects the top, bottom, and sides. Part of the bell has rusted right away, and the rest is rough and pitted like any piece of iron which has been left out in the rain for many years and then carefully cleaned and preserved. With the exceptioi. of their shrines, all these iron bells are crudely made, and if they have a clapper make the most lugubrious clonking noise. More musical and far more beautiful are the Irish bronze bells. These have curved handles, and inside at the top two iron stubs, the remains of a staple for the clapper projecting from the bronze. They are made in the same shape as the iron bells, rectangular in section, wide at the mouth and narrowing gradually towards the handle. But there is one exception, the bell of St. Cuana of Kilshanny in County Clare, which is circular like an inverted bronze bowl; it closely resembles a telephone bell and makes much the same noise.

The most beautiful of all the bronze bells in the British Museum is one which was found in Tyrone in 1832. It is very much later than all the others, Middle as opposed to Dark ages. The outside is as smooth as polished stone and is the colour of basalt. This bell is struck by a bronze ball attached by a piece of cord, and besides being unique for its beauty, it is also the only bronze bell to be truly tuneful, giving out a clear note and not the dull cow-bell noise. The only ugly bronze bell, stiff and cumbersome, with no subtlety of line, was dug up in a bog in County Leitrim. Two holes at the top are probably for the staple, and two projecting lumps of bronze may be the remains of a handle.

When the Church became firmly established these small bells fell out of use, although they continued to be rung in front of the Host on its way to the houses of the sick. There must also have been those wheels of small bells which are still rung in Spain and some parts of Germany at the elevation of the Sacrament in Roman Catholic churches; for Aubrey in the seventeenth century spoke to a man whose father had died at the age of 104 and who remembered that, before the Reformation, a wheel with eighteen bells attached to it used to be rung at Broken-borough church in Wiltshire. But the clergy now wanted large bells which could be heard over a wide area, ringing at the canonical hours, and by their size and sonority proclaiming the splendour of their church.

Bede, describing the death of the Abbess Hilda of Whitby in 680, says that the bells tolling for her could be heard thirteen miles away, though this may be considered miraculous by him and not necessarily refer to large bells. Croyland Abbey in 960 had six bells with fine resonant names, Bartholomew, Betelin, Turketyl, Tatwin, Pega, and Bega, and later Canterbury had five, needing eight men to ring the lightest and twenty-four the heaviest. The size of the bells was increasing and also the number; for though cathedral churches were only supposed to have seven bells and parish churches no more than three, this rule was not kept very strictly. Unfortunately no Saxon or Norman bells survive in England, but there are a few from the thirteenth century, and from this date we are no longer dependent on Ireland.

The great number of people needed to ring the bells at Canterbury gives an indication of how these first large bells were rung. The frontispiece of the belfry at Marston Moreteine in Bedfordshire, shows seventeenth century bells. Medieval bells would have been taller and would not have had whole wheels; otherwise from the thirteenth century on there has been very little change. Today canons, the metal hoops at the top by which the bell in the drawing is fixed to its headstock, are rarely used, but apart from that and such improvements as ball-bearings and cast-iron headstocks, the relation between bell, headstock, frame, and bearings were the same in the Middle Ages as they are now; what has changed is the way in which the bells are rung. On the Continent very heavy bells have a treading plank or board fixed across the headstock at right angles to it, and a number of men with one foot on the bell frame and the other on the board work it up and down like a see-saw, swinging the bell to and fro. This is probably the reason for the twenty-four men ringing the heaviest bell at Canterbury; the only other explanation, but a dubious one, is that the rope from the bell was arranged through a pulley so that it lay horizontally and the men pulled it as in a tug-of-war.

In England there are five ways of ringing a bell. The first is *clocking*: a rope is tied to the flight of the clapper

6

and the clapper pulled against the side of the bell, which hangs still. This has the great disadvantage that sooner or later the bell is bound to crack, and may be why so few of the earliest bells survive, for the difficulty of ringing the really heavy ones was so great that the easiest way sooner or later destroyed them. In 1594 the churchwardens of St. Lawrence's Church, Reading, made this resolution: "Whereas there was through the slothfulness of ye sexton in times past a kind of tolling ye bell by ye clapper rope; it was now forbidden and taken away and that the bell should be tolled as in times past and not in any such idle sort." This system is still used in churches where the frame is in such a state of disrepair that the bells cannot be swung round and there are no chiming hammers. *Chiming* the bell is hitting the soundbow, not with the clapper, but with a hammer, controlled by a rope, pulled either by hand or by machine. Again the bell does not move, but there is less danger of cracking it. If the bell is to be rung as well, the hammer can be fitted so that it will not interfere with the swinging of the bell. The third way of sounding a bell is confusingly also called *chiming*. The bell is swung a little and as it swings back the rope is checked and pulled again; the bell stops suddenly, but the clapper goes on and strikes the bell as it is pulled back. If this is done in slow time it is known as *tolling*.

Lastly there is *ringing* the bell, swinging it from side to side. The problem which medieval bell-hangers had to overcome was that of enabling the ringer to exert as much leverage as possible on the headstock, and their first solution was to fix a spar of wood at right angles to it, with the bell rope tied to the end. The longer the spar the greater the leverage. Naturally this method had the disadvantage that only when the spar was horizontal would the leverage be at its maximum, for the bell as it swung to and fro tilted the spar up and down, and moved the rope nearer to the headstock; in the same way that a fisherman, when looking at his bait, holds the rod straight

7

up and down, so that the line hangs straight down close in front of his nose, whereas when he lowers the rod towards the horizontal the line gradually moves farther away from him; the bell rope moving like the fishing line decreased the force exerted by the ringer. The next idea was to fix at the end of the spar a quarter circle of wood curving back towards the bell, like a segment of a cart wheel with a grooved rim to take the rope; this at least kept the rope at a constant distance from the headstock for part of the bell's swing, but only when the wheel was moving upwards. Then another quarter wheel was placed *on top* of the spar making a half wheel; the rope was attached to the rim directly above the headstock, and the original spar became a spoke supporting the rim of the wheel. The bell could now swing through a half-circle, with the leverage constant throughout its course. These half-wheels survived well into the last century, and three are preserved at Satterleigh in Devonshire.

The last invention was the whole wheel. With this the bell can be made to swing through a complete circle, and it will sound with its full note and tone because the clapper will strike it with maximum force. Ringing a bell with a whole wheel is very like sending up a child on a swing: from the vertical it will swing forward and upward, then drop back again, and rise up backwards before beginning to move again towards the vertical. It can only be pushed again just before it begins to drop forward; one *can* start a swing by pulling the child backward, but not for very far because its weight has to be lifted, so the easiest way is to implement the natural pendulum swing. So for the ringer; who stands with the sally level with his head and with the tail of the rope in his left hand; the bell is in position I on the diagram, and after the first pull or "sway" will rise to position II, and then start to drop back again like the child on the swing. As the bell passes the vertical it starts to wind up the rope on the rim of the wheel, and when it has risen as high as it can, the ringer gives another

8

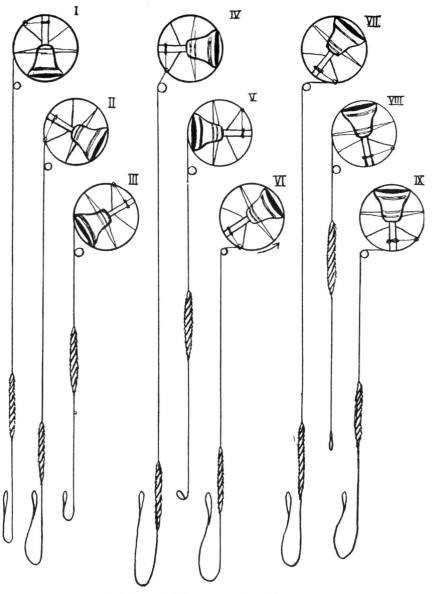

Raising a bell (see pages 8 and 10)

pull in position III; this time the bell moves higher, unwinding the rope as it swings till it stops in position IV. Again the ringer cannot pull while it is like this, but waits till it has moved back to position V, when a considerable amount of rope has been taken up on the wheel and the sally has passed out of reach, and he has to pull on the bight between the end of the sally and the tail. His leverage on the bell has now greatly increased, and the bell swings round, through position VI, with the rope being drawn over the ground pulley as it swings round till it reaches position VII. Between V and VI the rope has been hanging straight down beside the pulley, but between VI and VII after the garter hole has passed over the pulley, the sally begins to rise, and now that the rope has been drawn over the pulley, the ringer can pull on the bell when it is moving both ways, and increase its swing still further, so that this time it will move right up to VIII and be almost upside down, with the ringer holding on to the end of the rope.

The pull from VIII with the tail of the rope is called backstroke; the pull from IX with the sally is handstroke, and this alternation of backstroke and handstroke continues throughout the ringing. Getting the stationary bell "up" till it swings through the full circle from handstroke to backstroke is called "raising". Once it is raised, the bell can be "set" with its mouth upwards by allowing it to move gently past the point of balance as at IX when the stay will come up against the slider and hold the bell there. The bell can be lowered by checking its movement at handstroke and backstroke, so that its swing decreases till it is stationary and silent, hanging mouth downwards. *Firing* is ringing all the bells in a ring together at handstroke or backstroke so that they strike with one gorgeous clang. There is no definite date for the introduction of the whole wheel; the most likely time was during the sixteenth and seventeenth centuries, for it is then that the first references occur to change ringing, which is entirely dependent on the control of the bell, only achieved with a whole wheel. This invention had a profound influence on the ringing of bells, their shape, and the conduct of life in the belfry.

Although no Saxon or Norman bells survive, bells of the thirteenth, fourteenth, and fifteenth centuries still hang in a few churches of practically every English county. The earliest of these is, on the evidence of the lettering, the Hour Bell at Gloucester Cathedral; it bears stamped on it the arms of the abbey, St. Peter's crossed keys, and the founder's mark (a shield with three bells), and the inscription, "Me Fecit Fieri Conventus Nomine Petri". It is called Big Peter and used to hang in the choir, and be rung by eight or nine men; but now it is only chimed, for fear of damage. The first bell left to us bearing a date, 1296, is at Claughton in Lancashire, but at Caversfield in Oxfordshire there is a bell which was presented by Hugh Gargate, the lord of the manor, who died in 1219. Until the Reformation, bells were dedicated to the saints, Christ, the angels, and to the Virgin. The tenor, loudest and largest, was often named after the saint to whom the church was dedicated, and the others to each saint whose consecrated altar stood in the church below.

The dedicatory inscriptions on these pre-Reformation bells vary from the simple "Sancte Thomæ ora pro nobis", to the smarter hexameters of the fifteenth-century founders of Norwich, who would put "Virgo coronata, duc nos ad regna beata" on a bell dedicated to the Virgin. The tradition of giving a name to a bell dates from these dedications, a bell being called Luke or Agatha after its pious namesake, but often the name would commemorate a donor or some celebrity who was in no way a saint. The bells which can be called by some saintly name are rare. Generally they bear some pious or profane line which gives no opportunity for those who love familiarity to refer to "old Magdalen" when talking about a particular bell in their church, and the number of these old bells decreases yearly as more and more are recast.

11

Before the Reformation, church bells were dedicated in the same way as any other artifact used by the Church, and the service was similar to the Roman Catholic rite of the present day. The bell is washed with holy water, marked with the sign of the cross in oil while the bishop consecrates it and gives it a name, and then the censer is placed underneath so that it may be sweetened with incense. Eighteenth-century England took full advantage of the slumbering Established Church, and made the ceremony more convivial if less reverent. In 1735 the three old bells of Selborne were recast to make four, and Sir Simeon Stuart gave a fifth bell, dedicated to his favourite daughter. Gilbert White describes the consecration:

"The day of the arrival of this tuneable peal was observed as a high festival by the village, and rendered more joyous by an order from the donor that the treble bell should be fixed, bottom upwards in the ground, and filled with punch of which all persons were permitted to partake."

Dr. Alfred Gatty in *The Bell*, published in 1847, describes a similar service at Ecclesfield in South Yorkshire:

"Two wagons, decorated with boughs of evergreens and drawn by teams of grey horses bedizened with ribbons, set out for the merry peal and returned in the fine afternoon with their welcome load. The shouts of the multitude greet their arrival, and at the ancient public-house on the village green, the procession comes to a stand. Then commence the profane christenings. In one of the bells which has been inverted for the purpose, mine host mixes a motley compound of beer, rum, etc., which is liberally dispensed to the good-humoured bystanders. The Bell Founders' representative is busy on the occasion, and in the treble has a more delicate mixture from which he offers a libation to the more distinguished persons of the company."

In the nineteenth century the forms of service used by the Church of England were first introduced, and special hymns were written for these occasions; the Rev. J. M. Neale wrote one, which has this lovely verse:

12

And, when evening shadows soften
Chancel cross and tower and aisle;
It shall blend its vesper summons
With the day's departing smile.

Nowadays the great wave of interest in our parish churches has passed and the emphasis is on country houses. The church is still recognised by the picture postcards in the village post office, but it will have to compete with every imaginable view of the local piece of Adam, Kent, or Wyatt. Perhaps one reason for this change is the motor-car. There are few parts of England where there is not one church within five miles of another, forming a comfortable chain of rests for a cyclist or walker, but in the second motoring age when those lovely cars on the covers of early Ordnance Survey maps bowled past the pines of Surrey and over Salisbury Plain, the view was the thing and architecture was pushed into the background. Now the black beetles rush from ducal to baronial establishment, taking no notice of the churches except when they are very special. But a hundred years ago parish churches were the rage—any one of them was bound to have some interesting old bit which could be rubbed with heel-ball, or focused on the ground-glass screen of a fine brass-bound camera.

Many of these Victorian archæologists became experts on bells, and called themselves campanologists. They were dedicated to a much more frustrating and difficult art than the monumental brass rubbers. Rarely is the inscription on a medieval bell as crisp as the firmly incised lines on a brass plate. Also the part bearing the inscription tapers slightly, so the piece of paper always tends to slip upwards, making it difficult to keep it in place, even while it is being rubbed quite gently. All this means climbing backwards and forwards from one side of the bell to the other, getting very hot and dirty, covering one's clothes with oil from the bearings, and meeting the additional hazards of bats, bird droppings, and darkness. Then when the rubbing is

13

made and deciphered, the inscription may be of little interest and of little æsthetic value.

The medieval bell-founder was primarily concerned to cast a bell with a good tone, and before the scientific study of their shape, his greatest art lay in making bells which were in tune with each other. Rarely have founders in this country put on to their bells letters or marks which are first rate, though they are always of archæological interest, or charming or comic; decoration was of secondary importance, and so it is today. Some medieval inscriptions have been lost, because the bells have been recast, but we can still find others in the records of the campanologists. Their collections of rubbings, long strips of paper, tightly rolled and tied with pink tape, survive in libraries and museums, perhaps a trifle blurred yet retaining the vague outline of the letters and founders marks. Nineteenth-century books on bells are illustrated with engravings or lithographs of these inscriptions, nicely tidied up and giving no indication of their generally battered condition. Later, photography attempted to record them though with little success, for often they are so slightly raised and there is so little contrast of tone, that only the most skilful lighting will give a photograph with emotional as well as factual value.

The arrangement of the dedication on a medieval bell usually followed a closely set pattern: first the initial cross, seldom simple like the cross patty or crosslet of heraldry, but more elaborate, covered with formal foliated pattern. The words of the inscription came next in Gothic or Lombardic lettering, plain or ornamented. The most common ornament was to set a crown above each letter, particularly with Lombardic letters; others had the counters filled with ornament. Stephen Norton of Kent had one of the most elegant sets of letters for his inscriptions, crowned with a motif of fleurs-de-lys and balls, like a coronet, and the counter filled in with flowers. Somercotes in Lincolnshire has bells bearing elaborate capitals with grotesque faces

14

and figures in the counter. This is perhaps the most beautiful of the medieval founders alphabets. Several letters, the initial cross and the stop from it are at the head of this chapter. The words of the inscription were divided one from another by stops. There are many forms of these, though the initial cross might be used again here, or any stamp which the founder thought suitable. Stephen Norton had a prettily designed stop, tall and thin, crowned like his letters with fleurs-de-lys, and the body made of alternate quatrefoils and fleur-de-lys. Few founders' letters were of this standard, practically all their Lombardic being weak and wandering, and their Gothic crude.

Occasionally the letters making a word were broken into groups with stops, like the captions to the simpler stories in comics—"and how those per-ky pus-sies gig-gled to see Whis-kers with-out her bon-net". Tricks like this and frequent abbreviations—Pte for Peter—make deciphering difficult. The inscription was completed with the founder's mark; these are unreliable evidence for dating a bell, because in a great many cases the same mark was used by a foundry for many years.

Some founders, if they were not given an inscription, would fill in the space on the bell with letters of the alphabet. Others would stamp the mould with any mark to fill up an awkward gap. A number of churches in Gloucestershire have bells stamped with the portraits of a king, who has a beard like the tines of a fork pressed close together, and of a queen. These are supposed to represent Edward I and Eleanor of Castile. Coins were also used for a similar purpose, and are an indication of the date when the bell was cast. Later, in the seventeenth century, satirical medals, bearing such witty devices as a head which, looked at one way up, was a crowned king and the other way a triple crowned pope, became popular, and founders used them as stamps. But the medieval jokes were of the strictly Gothic kind, little grimacing faces, men with no body between neck and legs, lions' masks with fat protruding tongues, and other *niddy-noddy* grotesques. The whole design would often be enriched above and below the inscription with a decoration of leaves; grapes were a favourite motif, or perhaps some abstract ornament.

Despite the ablution with holy water, the anointing, and the censing, and the great sanctity of these medieval bells, with their sonorous dedications to the saints, they carried inscriptions which show that the clergy and the founders advertised the superiority of their possessions and products with the *naïveté* of the warranted, guaranteed, "none genuine without this signature", spirit of later English commerce. One common belief was that the sound of bells drove away thunder as well as devils, and East Anglian bells occasionally have stamped on them a fylfot or swastika, which, being the ancient badge of Thor, the god of thunder, kept him out of the parish. "Voce mea viva depello cuncta nociva"—"By my lively voice I drive away all harmful things"—refers to the belief that the sound of bells would drive away evil spirits. The leonine verse, in which the word before the caesura rhymes with the last word in the line, was the favourite medium of these early advertisements, and their simple rhymes, have been common to English bell inscriptions ever since.

There was a common leonine inscription for a founder who wished to assert his superiority, and this is the fore-runner of those doggerel rhymes which show so clearly the local rivalries between founders in the eighteenth and early nineteenth centuries, when it was still possible for a small firm to find sufficient work in quite a limited area of one county. "Me melior vere non est campana sub ere"—"A better bell than I cannot truly be found under the sky."

In England there is only one bell bearing an inscription in Norman French, but a founder would have been unlikely to use this language for an inscription; as he would be closely supervised by the ecclesiastics whose literary language was Latin. This case of the tenor at Bitterley in

16

Shropshire, cast by a Worcestershire bell founder early in the fifteenth century, may be due to the idiosyncrasy of the donor, Alice Sturye, which made her have her bell inscribed:

IEƧU . LEƧEIGNE . ƧEYNT . ANNE . PERLE
ORDYNAUNCE . ALEIƧƧTURYE . QUEDIU
AƧOILE . PURƧA GAUNT . MERCY

H. B. Walters translates this as: (dedicated to) The Lord Jesus (and) Saint Anne by the ordinance of Alice Sturye, whom God pardon by His great mercy. All the S's are reversed, and between the words are the king's heads referred to above, and between Seynt and Anne, the head of the queen; they are represented here by full stops.

There is another unique bell belonging to the late middle ages, it is an inch high replica of a church bell, said to have been worn by a pilgrim as proof of his pilgrimage to Canterbury. It is in the British Museum, and called Sancti Tomaes; it is a souvenir, the medieval equivalent of a model of the Eddystone lighthouse made of stone from Kynance Cove.

Before long two influences—the Reformation and the whole wheel—were to destroy both the medieval convention for inscriptions and also the actual bells themselves. After the Reformation bells were no longer consecrated. Instead of being suspended over censers they were used as great punchbowls, and this secularisation had its particular effect on the inscriptions. The sack of religious houses by Thomas Cromwell, and later the iconoclasm of men like the Protector Somerset, who built Somerset House from the profits he made pillaging chantry chapels, set a fine example to any patron of a church who wished to make money by selling the bell metal. Henry VIII sold a hundred thousand pounds avoirdupois to one dealer in monastic surplus stores. The destruction was so great that the commissioners sent out to make inventories of church property in 1549 were ordered to remind churchwardens that they were responsible for the safety of the bells. When Elizabeth I succeeded Mary, images and bells were once more taken down and sold, and in the second year of her reign she issued a proclamation to stop the sale of bells.

The whole wheel's influence was mechanical. Medieval bells were much taller and heavier than their present-day equivalents; the metal was thicker and the vertical distance from shoulder to sound bow greater than it is now. As a result, the bells were hard to ring because of the greater moment of the bell on the stock when the bell was horizontal. This could be counteracted by tucking the bell up into the headstock, so that the centre of gravity of the bell lay closer to the line of the bearings. When whole wheels were fitted to headstocks, it was found that shorter bells turned round much more easily than long ones, and there was accordingly an immediate change in fashion from the tall, thick, heavy bell to a short, thin, lighter bell, which could be rung with greater ease and precision. One result of this change was that the new bells had a much lighter tone. Great Tom of Christchurch, Oxford, was bought from Osney Abbey at the Dissolution, and before it was recast in 1612 bore this inscription: "In Thomæ Laude Resono Bim Bom Sine Fraude." Bim Bom is the difference; we now say ding dong, a tinny clanking description of a bell's note. Bim Bom is much richer and deeper, but besides onomatopœia, there is the evidence of medieval bells on the Continent, where more have survived and where their tone tends to be more mellow than our own later bells.

English became established as the language for bell inscriptions in the seventeenth century, but Latin continued for the smugger, more pious sentiments, and at the end of the sixteenth century a founder might still use a fairly elaborate verse such as:

Jubilate Deo Salvatori nostro
Cantabo laudes tuas Domine.

18

After this there were fewer Latin bell inscriptions, and the lull lasted for nearly three hundred years. Any memory of the Church of Rome was distrusted, and so the convention of dedicating to a saint lapsed until its revival by the Puseyites in the last century, when "Ave Sancta Trinitas, Ave Pax et Charitas" was placed on bells in rich illegible Gothic in 1845. Since that date many clergymen have used Latin inscriptions which, though asserting their isolation in a cosy world where Lewis and Short is close by on the shelf, are of little comfort to many ringers, or to those amateur archæologists who get into a belfry with no more sinister intention than that of discovering what is written on the bells. Few of the scanty Latin inscriptions on bells for the last four hundred years are amusing or throw any light on contemporary history; most just echo the embalmed beliefs of the people who wrote or selected them, "Invoco in templum domini" for the seventeenth century, and "Sum vox clamantis præparate viam domini" for the eighteenth, revived Popish for the nineteenth and uninspired English translated into Latin for the twentieth. All dull with one exception; Bishop's Morchard, a sensible Devon village, in 1743 inscribed a bell "Floreat Bishop's Morchard".

The best bell inscriptions of the last three centuries are in English, and the best of these record more than just the names of the churchwardens, the rector, and the founder. They revive vividly the age in which they were composed. The lettering of the inscriptions on these post-Reformation bells is nearly always contemporary. Roman letters were used from the seventeenth century onwards, and correspond closely to any piece of seventeenth- or eighteenth-century lettering, whether on a tomb or a milestone, but never of a very high standard. Initial crosses were dropped and so were stops. One particularly interesting bell is at Tisbury in Wiltshire; it was cast by William Corr in 1700. There is no inscription other than two absurd initials, and a band of completely random ornament, resembling the calligraphic *tour de force* of the writing masters, curly and loose, cherubs' heads, little figures, and foliage. Gothic lettering had to wait till the nineteenth century to come back into favour, and then it was only used by the larger founders. *Art nouveau* also had a brief ascendancy over Roman, but now the punches are almost all Roman, clear, legible, but perhaps a trifle dull. It is a pity that bell founding did not succumb to the Victorian movement of florid lettering, but the influence of the Ecclesiological Society was too strong.

Most English inscriptions either tell something of the bell's history or express some pious or profane sentiment, and very few will be found which do not fall into one of these two categories. One of the earliest inscriptions in English, 1595, is "Embrace Trew Museck"; during the eighteenth and early nineteenth centuries this was a constant theme.

> *How has the chirping treable sounds so clear*
> *While rowling Tom comes tumbling in the reare.*
>
> (1732)

The onomatopœic word "bom", in the tradition of Great Tom of Christchurch's original inscription, is altered to rhyme very nicely in this verse:

> *That all may come and none may stay at home*
> *I ring to sermon with a lusty bome.*

The tradition of inscribing the treble "Glory be to God in the highest", the second bell "And in earth peace", and the third "Goodwill towards men", was adapted for the music made by a ring cast in 1710. "Musick is not worth a groate" on the treble; "But yet musick won't agree unless tis seconded by me" for the second; and the tenor, "Yet all is a confused noise without my last commanding voice". Towards the end of that century Joseph Pizzie and William Gwynne gave a bell to Aldbourne Church which was cast

20

by Robert Wells in 1787, and to record their generosity they wrote this little rhyme and had it cast on the bell:

Music and ringing we like so well
And for that reason we gave this bell.

Pious inscriptions are usually well-known lines from the Bible or the liturgy, such as "Holy, Holy, Holy, Lord God of Sabaoth", or "Praise ye the Lord". The last spark of the eighteenth-century spirit flickered in 1885 when one bell had "True hearts and sound Bottoms" put on it; while one curate wrote this splendid verse for the tenor bell of a new ring in 1858:

We hang here to record
That the church was restored
In the year of our lord 1858.

Lord let the folk below
Resound with living song
Thy praise, as we do now
With iron Tongue.

There are traditional verses for the tenor, referring to its use as a passing bell:

I sound to bed the sick repent,
In hope of life when breath is spent
(1660)

I sweetly tolling men do call
To taste of meats to feed the soul.
(late 17th century)

And very common indeed:

I call the quick to church and dead to grave.

Another version combining the same thought and recording a gift is at Walmsley in Lancashire:

At the age of twenty and three,
Samuel Isherwood gave me
That to church I might call thee
(1882)

BIE-C

21

These rhymes recording the generosity of a donor become more and more pompous with time; in 1700:

> *All you of Bath that hear me sound*
> *Thank Lady Hopton's hundred pound.*

Then in 1827:

> *Squire Arundel the great my whole expense did raise,*
> *Nor shall our tongues abate to celebrate his praise.*

And the most extreme case of all, that of the seventh and eighth at Arundel cast in 1855, which bore below the arms of the Duke of Norfolk this inscription:

> *The most high potent and most ˙noble prince Henry*
> *Charles Duke of Norfolk, Earl Marshall, and*
> *hereditary Marshall of England, Earl of Arundel,*
> *Surrey, and Norfolk, Baron Fitz-Alan Clun and*
> *Oswaldestre, and Maltravers, Knight of the most*
> *ˌNoble Order of the Garter.*

Many inscriptions celebrate the ringing of bells for weddings:

> *When female virtue weds with manly worth*
> *We ring with rapture and we spread it forth.*

Now spangled wedding bells are symbols for marital bliss, honeymoons, hired cars with white ribbons, and special, silver-printed stationery.

In 1815 Mad Jack Fuller, the noted eccentric who lived at Brightling in Sussex, recast the five old bells of the church and gave a new treble. Three years later he gave two more. All were made by Mears of Whitechapel. The treble and second bell were called Waterloo, and the second has this inscription: "This peal of bells was completed A.D. 1818 at the expense of John Fuller." The third was called Ta:.vera, the fourth Salamanca, the fifth

Vittoria, the sixth Pyrenees, the seventh Orthes, and the eighth Tolouse, with the inscription: "The five bells recast and a new treble added at the expense of John Fuller Esq late member of the county 1815, in honour of the Illustrious Duke of Wellington his last six victories are here recorded." Fuller increased the number of bells in his parish church by recasting and he also gave a barrel organ and a set of bassoons. In 1701 at another church:

> *John Gilberd did contrive*
> *To cast from four this peal of five.*

These are two examples of the vast number of bells made or recast in the two centuries from 1660 to 1860. Later work is more restoration than creation.

When the whole wheel was invented and it became possible to control a bell, ringing rounds—ringing the bells in order from treble to tenor—became popular; soon change ringing was invented, altering the order in which they rang each time the bells moved. Change ringing is based on permutation, the more bells the greater the number of times they can be rung in a different sequence. Change ringing will be explained in greater detail in a later chapter, but it is sufficient to say now that the greater the number of bells the happier a change ringer will be. All over the country the old rings of three bells, the greatest number which the canons allowed a parish church, were taken down and recast into four; more were added by the generosity of squires or ringers. Often when new bells were added the old ones were not recast and the old treble would become number two or four. It is naturally cheaper to make light bells than heavy ones, and further, if the frame had no room for more bells, the new ones would have to be put on top of the old frame, which would not be practicable with a very heavy bell. Today there are only three foundries in the whole country, but during the period of expansion there were small foundries all over England, competing fiercely with each other.

Bilbie and Boosh may come and see
What Evans and Nott have done by me.
(1758)

said Evans and Nott of a rival, and

Before I was a broke I was as good as any
But when Cokey casted I near was worth a penny.
(1732)

said the slandered Bilbie about another rival.

One of the greatest arts of the founder was to cast bells in tune with each other. There was a rough-and-ready method of calculating the weight of metal needed, but it was entirely a matter of judgment and not an exact rule, as it is now; so the founder who put upon a bell the inscription:

I am little smart and small
Luck made me concord to all.

was counting his chickens before they were hatched, since the inscription is placed on the mould before the bell is cast. Davis, too, counted his chickens when he used this inscription:

Our sound is good our shape is neat,
It's Davis cast us so complete.

Luckily for him his bell was neither cracked nor out of tune.

Perhaps the most touching of all these inscriptions are those placed on the bells for a church at Glastonbury by T. Pyke of Bridgwater in 1776; for the treble:

Public subscription gave us birth,
Now our dear tones shall join in mirth.

And for the second:

Our tones would all have been much deeper
If contributions had been greater.

24

No one can possibly claim that English bell inscriptions are great poetry, but they do have the power to evoke that idea of eighteenth-century rustic life which we all have. A world of smocks, green grass, and earthenware mugs painted with sheaves of corn and pitchforks; not the real world of hunger and discomfort, where "Prosperity to this parish," "Let brotherly love continue" and "God preserve the King and prosper the trade of Northam" were heartfelt prayers to sound over the parish whenever the badger-legged ringers rang the bells on Sundays and holidays. Inscriptions of this century are dull because they commemorate events which are still too close, and a false conception of piety forbids us make our bells, for the delight of future generations, memorials of feuds, whist-drives, or jumble sales.

2

Tag-rags of the Village

THE great medieval bells, heavy and sonorous, hanging in their new white or golden stone belfries, were rung by men only superficially different from those who ring them today. Portraits show the same crabbed or happy faces, and the same concentration. King David, tapping out a tune on small bells inside the initial letter of the forty-sixth psalm in a manuscript, looks as contented as a small boy doing the same thing on the bells in a country house with a broom-stick. The bells and the method of ringing them may change with time, but the ringers remain the same.

Before the Reformation the religious houses and churches kept time for the people, and in an age of almost complete silence, except for the mumblings of humanity and animals, the deacons and clerks in minor orders divided the day by sounding the canonical hours at six in the morning for prime with one stroke, tierce at nine with three, at midday lauds with three, nones at three o'clock in the afternoon with three, and at six again vespers, when the bells rang many times. As well as these, there were others—the Gabriel bell in the morning and evening, the Pardon Bell before or after a service (anyone hearing it should say an Angelus), the Sanctus bell during Mass; and special occasions. For instance, when Bishop John of Ely consecrated a new ring in that cathedral on May 3rd, 1490, people who said five paternosters on hearing the great bell for the first time received forty days' indulgence.

The deacons and clerks had also to ring for a bishop visiting their church, and especially for an Archbishop of Canterbury, like Thomas of Arundel who, when he came to London, "took great snuff" that the bells of some churches were not rung in his honour, and promptly suspended them. Bishop Oldham in 1511 directed that Annualarii, priests who were solely employed in singing annuals and anniversary masses for the dead, were to ring first one bell, and then all the bells at the canonical hours, and then start the service. The whole course of life was ordered by these bells and by the actions performed at their sound.

Before the Reformation there were secular ringers besides the clergy, and the earliest recorded band were the members of the Guild of Ringers of Westminster. Henry III in 1224 ordered his Keeper of Works at Westminster to give a beam to the Abbot to support his bells, and thirty years later ordered that the members of the Guild who rang them were to be given one hundred shillings a year and allowed the privileges and customs which they had exercised since the reign of Edward the Confessor. Nearly a hundred years later Edward III built at Westminster a "strong clochard of stone and timber covered with lead", which held three bells, and though there is no connection between the ringers of these and the Guild of Westminster, when Stow says they rang "at coronations, triumphs, funerals of princes and their obits", there is a suggestion that laymen and not clergy pulled the ropes.

The records of other English guilds show again the development of laymen as ringers. At Stamford in 1494 the Guild of St. Katherine reaffirmed its rules which the prologue suggests were in use for a considerable time before that date. On the Sunday after the Feast Day of their Patron Saint the members held a dinner; when the bell of St. Paul's Church was knelled, "all brothers and sisters of the Guild shall come into the Hall and dine together"; and on the same day, in the afternoon, a "Placebo and Dirige" was to be said in the same Church for all the deceased members of the Guild, "and there to ring III peals; with Mass of Requiem on the next morrow, with as many peals". Afterwards the Steward of the Guild gave the ringers bread and cheese and drink, the clerk for his ringing twopence, the bellman one penny and bread and cheese and drink. The ordinances of several guilds mention the bellman, an official who is now only a memory and a myth, to be discussed in a later chapter.

The Guild of Tailors of Exeter in 1483 decided that they should give fourpence to the ringers on the anniversary of the death of their late master, John Hamelyn, for ringing at a Requiem and Dirige. Always the anniversaries of death were to be remembered with the sound of bells, but in another hundred years the comfortable system which provided for the peace of the dead was broken up. Many of the monuments and works of art which the Church had given to this country were destroyed, and the smooth machinery of Requiem and Dirige, and the ritual tolling of bells to the memory of past-masters and members which was to have continued till the Day of Judgment, was stopped. The ringers after the Reformation became exclusively secular, and not until the nineteenth century were the clergy forced to bother themselves about the ringing of their bells.

After the Reformation the history of English bell ringers becomes clearer; we are no longer dependent for information upon the directives of bishops and priests, nor upon the murky evidence of parish accounts recording "to sexton 5d for ringing at the king's crownation", or for "monies spent on beare for a peele" to celebrate a victory on land or sea. The light of the Renaissance illuminates the scene, and with it comes the urge, still so fundamental to the social life of this country, to found societies, to join together, so that some idiosyncrasy common to a few people can be fostered with comfort, lost causes revitalised, forgotten or useless crafts, long dead from a combination of old age and economics, relearnt, and tin huts and large stone buildings consecrated to the study of these arts. The first sign of this new regimentation of knowledge to affect bell ringing is found in the rules of the Society of Saint Stephen's Ringers of Bristol. The earliest copy of these is dated 1620, but Toulmin Smith considers that the society was in existence before that date.

Before this, with the exception of the Ringers of Westminster, bell ringing was incidental to guild life. The Saddlers held the right to ring the bells of St. Martin le Grand, but they were not exclusively concerned with ringing. Other Guilds used bells only in the normal course of their religious life, but the Bristol society was formed solely to pursue the art of ringing. When the religious houses were destroyed and when the discipline surrounding the performance of religion relaxed, it became fashionable to ring the bells of the churches as a sport. This was practised by anyone who had the inclination, and naturally led to the formation of groups of men who had a jargon and symbolism in common, and they made codes of conduct, enforcing elaborate elections, and disciplinary fines to organise their sport satisfactorily.

The rules of the Society of Saint Stephen are similar to the rules which govern a professional society today, defining the objects of the society and the qualifications for membership. For them, members must be honest, clean-living people, prepared to defend the Society against contumely or ridicule: "so that we may not only stop the mouths of those that would or shall exasperate themselves against us, but also gain credit and reputation by our musical exercises; that others of our rich neighbours, hearing these loud cymbals with their ears may by the sweet harmony thereof be enlarged in their hearts, to pull one string to make it more sweet".

Next, there are the rules for the election of the Society's officers. The Master was to be elected from three candidates nominated, and the two Wardens from four nominated members. Four meetings of the Society were to be held every year, and the membership fee of fourpence per annum was to be paid at these meetings in penny parts, and every member who failed to pay was to be fined threepence. The election of Master took place every Michaelmas between five and eight o'clock in the morning, when the Wardens were to remind members of this meeting. On his election, the Master had either to give the members of the Society a breakfast or pay two shillings to the funds; in return the Wardens gave him a pint of wine apiece.

The rest of the rules lay down the activities of the Society. The Master was responsible for seeing that the members rang a peal every fortnight, and that while they were doing this any cursing, swearing, noise, or disturbance was punished with a fine of threepence. In the ringing chamber the members must choose which bell they would pull in strict seniority of membership, and anyone "saucey enough to take a rope before the Master and the next senior members have decided where they shall ring, 2d. fine".

The next rule is to preserve the ringing chamber and the ringers from the local bumpkins. Anybody who came into the tower and saw that circle of earnest dedicated faces, and found the sight comic, was immediately fined threepence. There was a case recently of a somewhat similar kind. A clergyman was promoted to a deanery, and a peal was rung in the tower of his church in his honour; a long, intricate, change-ringing peal, maintaining the strict and intricate movement of each bell against the others and calling for a great deal of concentration. (If the five thousand odd changes which make a true peal for change ringers is spoilt in any way, about three hours' work is wasted, and all their labour comes to nothing.) Just when the ringers had nearly succeeded, the vicar came into the church tower and disturbed them, so that the flawless mirror of sound which they had been making to celebrate his promotion was cracked. Alas.

The remaining rules are orders for ringing peals on the anniversaries of the deaths of members who left money to the Society. If the Master failed to remind the members that the dead were to be honoured in this way, he was to be fined.

The Society still prospers, and the minute books record its history with but one short break. An ordinance of November 17th, 1701, is interesting because it is one of the earliest accounts of a society's annual dinner, the yearly frolic, when a distinguished guest makes a fine after-dinner speech, and frustrated members get together in corners and plan the great schism which is to burst upon the unhappy committee at the next general meeting. This ordinance decrees that: "This day agreed that whereas a Bean Feast is annually held for ye Society of Ringers, that every person of the Society, being personally warned, and not giving a sufficient excuse to be allowed off by ye Society for his not appearing at the feast, shall pay for such default one shilling, to be applied towards ye discharge of ye said feast." However dull the dinner now, nobody is fined for not going. At the beginning of the last century the knells were still rung for past members, but

31

greater attention was paid to the Bean Feasts than to ringing, and a newspaper report of 1822 says that they sang glees and catches after dinner and that the *real ringers* played a peal on handbells. During the 1870s the Rector suggested that their concern should be for the restoration of the church, and they succeeded in raising vast sums of money for this purpose from the wealthy and distinguished membership. One venture was, however, not so successful; they decided to give a new pulpit, and substituted for the old baroque one a fine piece of ecclesiological carving in alabaster. Parts of the baroque pulpit were turned into a splendid chair for the Master of the Society; but after a few years they admitted that it was uncomfortable, and it was placed in the Red Lodge in Bristol.

These are the first rules for the conduct of a ringing society, but they are only one aspect of the moral code governing ringers. When ringing became a secular art, and even more especially when the conduct of ringers relaxed during the seventeenth and eighteenth centuries, rules were put up in churches to order their behaviour. Bell ringing as a sport had, and still has, little connection with the Church, and the tower is always devoid of any object to connect it with the altar. Change ringing and the improvements in bell hanging encouraged those people who, while not eager to ring a bell when some degree of muscular effort was needed, were only too willing to try when the bells turned round more easily.

The early change ringers were all men of that seventeenth-century cast of mind which eagerly attempted such experiments as the "killing of a frogge by dropping tar upon its head and back", or whether "hydropical persons swell most in the increment of the moone" and who enjoyed such a charming conceit as "Signor Verdero in a Burdock green hatt with an hattband of poppy leaf verts, set with emeralds and berylls and a plume of parret green feathers, and Pantoffles of cabbage colour laced with sea Holly or eryngo green"; or a dialogue "between two twins

32

in the womb concerning the world they were to come into"; that could write a Latin epigram on "a rich covetous person in Jaundis"; and who felt that "he that found out the line of the middle motion of the planets holds an higher mansion in my thoughts than he that discovered the Indies". This particular mind was an exception, but in the way that exceptions prove the grammatical rules, they also prove the rule of contemporary behaviour. No bell ringer has been as diverse or as intelligent as Sir Thomas Browne, but many of his contemporaries found in the intricate and certain mathematics of permutation a pleasure equivalent to such thoughts as his.

Members of such ringing societies as the Ancient Society of College Youths or the Society of Royal Cumberland Youths did not frolic about in church towers; they were far too interested in their art. But their less noble and less mathematically minded contemporaries found in the belfry a convenient club-house where they could work off the stored tedium of six days of village life with hard labour on the bell ropes, drink, and conversation; the early rules were attempts to restrain them.

At Scotter in Lincolnshire a poem over the door leading to the tower is clearly the clerk's ingratiating way of extracting money from the ringers:

> *Yow ringers all*
> *Who heare doe fall*
> *And doe cast over*
> *A bell doe forfeit*
> *To the clarke theirfore*
> *A growte I doe yow*
> *Tell and if yow*
> *Thinck it be to*
> *Little and beare*
> *A valiant minde*
> *Ye more yow give*
> *Unto him than*
> *Yow prove to him*
> *More kinde.*

33

Casting over a bell is pulling the rope so hard that the bell cannot be held by the stay, which breaks and the bell turns right over and gets out of control. It is always penalised in these doggerel rules with a small fine, and another set, which begins with the laudable exhortation, "Praise the Lord with Lowd Symbals" has a sixpenny fine:

> *If a bell you overthrow*
> *Sixpence is due before you go.*

The poetry is never of a high standard, and a few extracts will show their scope, although one is more elaborate than the others, it describes each offence, and the fines imposed are written down in a column opposite the appropriate verse in the poem, the poet deciding that it was far too difficult to find rhymes for pence or shillings for twenty odd couplets. All the other anonymous poets incorporate the amount of the fine into the verse, making doggerel of a bad but charming kind.

Spurs and hats were not worn by ringers. The rule against hats was understandable, but the ban on spurs seems unaccountable, though perhaps when a tyro had overthrown his bell and the rope was lashing about in the ringing chamber, it could catch some fine flash spur and pull boot and ringer up to the ceiling.

> *For wearing spurs or hat your forfeit is for that*
> *Just fourpence down to pay, or lose your hat.*

Swords and sword-belts were also bad form:

> *If you ring with gurse or belt*
> *We will have sixpence or your pelt.*

Disturbance and noise also:

> *If you chance to curse or sware*
> *Be sure you shall pay sixpence heare.*

The doggerel in another of these verses castigates any-

34

one unfortunate enough to lose his temper with another ringer, making him miss his stroke and mar the ringing.

All persons that disturbance here create
Forfeit one shilling towards the ringers treate.

A nice dialect rhyme, with a rich, greedy sound, eagerly collecting the fine with which to buy more bread, cheese, and drink. These rhymes, written with the vigour and crudity common to all vernacular poetry, show that there was some discipline in a minority of towers, but at a time when drunkenness was one of the few pleasures impoverished country labourers or artisans in the town could indulge, it is understandable that they spent on beer and gin any money earned for ringing, and were jealous of their supposed right to ring whenever they chose.

During the eighteenth and early nineteenth centuries the bells rang for the services; but they had a much wider application than they have now, and any festivity was an excuse for ringing—victories (after Trafalgar they rang peals for the victory and then death knells for Nelson), fairs, horse-races, and the Fifth of November were all celebrated with peals. One of the last occasions when the feeling of the people was expressed in this way was the successful outcome of the trial of Queen Caroline. *The Times,* from November 15th to 25th, 1820, besides having strangely modern advertisements for the sale of surplus clothing from the Napoleonic wars (a large parcel of Navy and Marine slops, including 2,500 red baize shirts), carried extensive reports of the rejoicing in various parts of the country.

Anyone who opposed the Queen was most unpopular, and the excitement became so great that at Malton, when the Bill of Pains and Penalties passed its second reading, the bells rang a muffled peal. The Marquess of Buckingham on his way home to Stowe was mobbed in Aylesbury, the postilions pulled off their horses, and only after more than an hour of booing was he able to continue his journey and leave the town "amidst the most deafening groans". At Stratford, Mr. Moss, a chemist, illuminated his shop with a C.R. and a crown in variegated lamps, much admired; but two people in Lymington whose relations held government appointments had all their windows broken for not illuminating. A clergyman in Hertford, who foolishly thought that this was the time to assert an Englishman's right to his own opinions, did not light his windows, and when the mob wanted to know why, came out of his front door armed with a blunderbuss.

> "Here sundry handfulls of well-directed mud, the argumenta lutone of his mottled congregation, effectually closed the mouth of the doughty orator, greeted and bespattered with the hooting of his victorious antagonists, the gospel trumpeter sounded his retreat to the smashing of his windows."

In other towns when the mail-coaches, the horses, and drivers, wearing a profusion of white ribbons, arrived bringing news of the trial, the first thing to do was to ring the bells. At Faringdon "many of the most respectable inhabitants ran towards the church and running up the belfry stairs, the bells instantly struck up a merry peal". Wolverhampton collected so much money for the ringers that they rang for a whole day incessantly, and the people of Darlington were well behaved, first asking the clergymen and churchwardens if they could use the bells. White flags were hung from many towers, and at night sheep were roasted in the streets. A green bag or the Italian witnesses in effigy were burnt on enormous bonfires of faggots, coal, tar, and oil. In Bristol many parishes, "where the inter-meddling of some officious and official party did not interfere to prevent the ebullition of popular joy, the church bells continued to ring merry peals".

In other towns meddling parties stopped the ringers. At Newport on the Isle of Wight the churchwardens felt that the bells should not ring, and dismissed the ringers just after they had started a peal, but influential people in the town interceded for them, and they went back to the tower to ring for the rest of the day and well into the night. In other places, if they were turned out of the tower, they rang handbells in the street, and at Sherborne in Dorset a magistrate would not allow the bells to ring, so the mob spent the day drinking and dancing outside his house, with great restraint not breaking his windows.

The authority of the clergy and wardens over the bells in the church tower was severely tested by the rejoicing after Queen Caroline's trial. The law is that before the bells can be rung the permission of the clergyman and wardens must be given, and they alone can say who shall ring and what shall be rung. But after a century and more when no one really cared what happened to the bells, the control of the tower passed to the ringers, and in the first part of the last century several cases were taken to court by rectors to prove that they and not the ringers controlled the tower. In 1830 the Rector of Chesterfield refused permission after he had been petitioned by the Mayor for the bells to ring for the races. The Rector of Mortehoe in Devon was locked out of the tower by one of the churchwardens, who nailed up the door, and D. Waite, a farmer of Thurnby, Leicestershire, broke open the door of the belfry so that he and the ringers could ring in honour of Lord Stamford, whose hunt was holding a meet in the village. In each case the court ruled that the clergy had absolute control over the ringing of the bells and that they should keep the keys of the belfry. At Chesterfield and Mortehoe no fines were imposed, but at Thurnby the ringers were fined; and when they refused to pay were sent to prison, and remained there for five weeks, till the fines were paid for them at the instigation of the rector.

When the Oxford Movement woke up the Church of England, clergymen, besides restoring their churches, turned their attention to the bells and the ringers. Both were found suffering from rot and neglect.

The Cambridge Camden Society, which later became the Ecclesiological Society, supervised the spring-cleaning of churches from 1839 to 1868. *The Ecclesiologist,* official organ of the society, has in it many articles on ringers and belfries. "Cantab. M.A.", writing in the sixties, gives a general account of the way in which bells were used at that time.

> "They are abused to assist the song of the drunkard and lend a kind of revel charm to a drunken and debauched bout as is alas far too often the case. The village fair, for instance, is not a fitting occasion for the bells in the tower of our church to pour forth their scientific melody, nor any of the mad holidays or drunken festivals which occur periodically in some villages."

When Ellacombe, the greatest Victorian campanologist, recorded the inscriptions on the bells of Devonshire—he visited every parish church in the county within twelve months—he found that in many places it was hardly safe to climb up the towers. The floor-boards were often rotten, the bells in a state of complete decay, broken, never rung and never repaired, and often so obscured with jackdaws' nests and guano that it was almost impossible to see them. He felt that the articles of inquiry from Rural Deans, Archdeacons, and Bishops about each parish should include questions on the state of the belfry, and the ringers, whether or not they smoked or drank in the ringing chamber, and if they held prize-ringing contests. Repairs to the belfry proved a much simpler matter than reforming the ringers, and those zealous clergymen to whom the credit must be given for preserving a great many of our parish churches had long and boring battles with the ringers.

Church bell ringers in country parishes were then noted for drunkenness and bigotry. To say "That man is a ringer" was to call him a drunkard, and another saying was that the number of bells in the tower equalled the number of drunks in the village. Ellacombe reported a case where a clergyman who could afford to be choosy refused a living when he found that there were bells in the tower, and one curate left his curacy because the ringers made his life a misery. The money they made ringing "spoilt them for two days or more"; one day they were drunk, and the next was spent recovering at home in bed. Ellacombe considered no other institution in a parish caused as much trouble and annoyance as the belfry and ringers. A letter in a number of *The Ecclesiologist* for 1865, recording the "Successful Tactics of a Country Curate with an Ungodly Set of Ringers", gives another account of these difficult men.

> "I have never been an eye-witness of the arcana of a belfry till I came to this parish. As you can readily conceive, Sir, I was terribly disgusted with what I witnessed; for the belfry on ringing nights was the regular resort of all the tag-rags of the village, who regarded the performance in the light of a jollification, instead of a 'hollification'."

This was the tradition which had to be broken, and many parsons set out to "snap the monotonous link which has bound together the Belfry and the Beer-house".

However, if the parsons wished for a reform, the ringers bitterly resented any interference with the privileges which they had established for themselves. The belfry was their club-house, and they were only too willing to start life-long feuds, beloved in villages even today, with anyone who interfered with their rights. "Cantab. M.A." reminds the readers of his article of "ringers' ignorant narrow-minded views on every moral subject, and that they impute to us similar motives to those which actuate themselves". One of the difficulties encountered by parsons was that if they were given a living where their predecessor had been lax in his supervision of the tower, the ringers often held the key, which they would never give back as it was their most powerful weapon in the battle. A parson who changed

39

the lock on the tower door and stopped ringing in this way would probably make the whole village so resentful that it would be impossible for him to attempt any other work for the improvement in the condition of his parishioners. So he had to plan his campaign with great care. On Sundays the bells were rung before the service, and the men would come down the tower and loll about in the churchyard till the service was over, and then go back and ring again. Sometimes ringing before church was just a convenient way of meeting before going off to the public-house for the rest of the day. No real progress could be made until the rector controlled the tower. Then the next move was to forbid ringing entirely on Sundays, but allow the ringers to practise on two evenings a week, the parson ringing the bells with them. Once he had shown them that good behaviour and ringing were not incompatible, a set of rules could be drawn up with a series of fines to enforce them, similar to the seventeenth- and eighteenth-century rules, but in fine Victorian prose, not doggerel; and every man would be made to sign a copy before becoming a member of the band. Even at this stage there were troubles;

> "The time to look out for a mutiny is when we forbid the use of the bells on some formerly allowed occasion, which used to be more than ordinarily productive of beer—such times as Whitsuntide, or when some famous cricket-match or horse-race comes off."

But one of the best ways of encouraging reform was to show the ringers' wives that if their husbands were members of an orderly band which did not drink, they would not have to deal with bilious and crotchety husbands the day after ringing.

One problem which had to be overcome, if it was necessary to forbid Sunday ringing, was to find a way of sounding the bells for the service. Ellacombe installed a specially designed set of chiming hammers, which could be worked by anyone, even a small boy. In this way the bells rang, but without allowing the unreformed ringers into the church. Another alteration which Ellacombe and other parsons advocated was that the bell ropes should come right down to the floor of the church, so that the ringers would not be in an isolated room up in the tower. In this way he felt that whatever respect they had for the altar would influence their conduct while they were ringing.

Harry B. Trelawney, in a lecture which he gave at Penzance in 1865 and also in a letter to *The Ecclesiologist* in 1864, had this to say about the ringers' behaviour. He was one of the few writers on the subject who, by implication, blamed the clergy for causing, through neglect and sloth, conditions which encouraged the ringers' tradition of drunkenness.

> "It is unskilful handling, clumsy positions, and the culpable neglect of the bells that make ringing laborious, and furnish an excuse for the everlasting beer-can."

He felt that if change ringing could be introduced into more towers, the men could be shown that their art was an intellectual as well as a physical exercise, and that a better kind of person would be attracted to the belfry. The curate whose tactics were successful with his ungodly ringers asked them to a supper on Christmas Eve, and when they were full of roast goose and plum pudding gave a short talk on the text that the belfry was no place to drink and smoke. Producing a set of rules for a proposed ringers' club, he asked them to elect a captain and treasurer and to make him a member, which they did. By ringing with them, his influence, and the pride which the ringers had in being members of a well-organised band, completed their reformation.

Now, after nearly a hundred years the work of the reformers is complete. The ringers are organised into Diocesan Guilds, and even if they are not members of a Guild, subscribing to its rules and discipline, it is no longer possible to say "that a man is a ringer therefore he is a drunk", but instead "that man is a ringer, therefore he is respectable". There would be no fear of an orgy if the bells were rung for a horse-race, and it seems strange that the Church of England, which is always seeking to establish itself in the lives of the people, should not allow the bells to ring more often than they do. In towns when the ringers practise in the evenings, people complain of the noise they make. If the Church had the courage to allow the bells to be rung on occasions which associated it with public rejoicing and pleasure, it could further achieve the end it seeks of a religion fused with every aspect of life. What could be nicer than to hear the bells ringing in a town whose team had returned victorious with the F.A. Cup, or listen to Westminster Abbey, St. Paul's and Southwark Cathedrals ringing a merry peal when leaving one of the Southern Railways termini on a Bank Holiday excursion? But the Church is too timid now.

The present generation of ringers behaves differently, but in most respects the men are similar to their nineteenth-century predecessors. In the towns their daily occupation may be anything, and their ringing interest lies in change ringing. In the country most of the ringers will be connected with the land, and in the West of England they will generally ring call changes. Although there are many ringers in the towns, we tend to discount them; when people who do not ring bells think of ringing at all, their thoughts immediately turn to that church tower poking above a ridge of dimly agricultural land. The only generalisation which can be made is that any band of ringers will be a fair cross-section of the community in that parish in the country or near that church in the town. One other factor has altered ringing—nowadays many more women are ringers than before the war.

The tower of a church is controlled by a steeple master if it is a grand one, but in smaller churches the captain will add to his tasks of organising the ringers the mechanical maintenance of the bells. He should also, some people feel, attend church after ringing for a service and be an example to others, but the dichotomy between ringing and religion is deep if erratic. Some ringers go to church, others do not, and where this is freely admitted, the parson being glad that his bells are well rung, and the ringer thankful for being allowed to ring, no one can feel resentful. Amongst the ringers in any parish there will often be a man whose known ancestors have rung the bells in the tower before him. Besides this tradition of families providing ringers for the church, ringers are bound together as a group in the community by the bond between them of a skill and knowledge, not common to the rest of society, in the way that doctors and lawyers are bound together. This means that new ringers are often recruited to the band because of a desire to be initiated in the esoteric mysteries of the belfry.

To see the ringers at work we must, for picturesque reasons, go to the country. The town has its own picturesque of gasometer, canal, smoke, and chimneys, but there are too many churches and bells sounding in competition, distracting our attention from one steeple; while in the country as soon as the bells from the single church start to ring, the tower becomes the focus of the parish. So to see the ringers of today we must seek out the clearer air and bumbly landscape of the English country parish.

On Sunday, about half an hour before the service for which the bells are to ring, the band assembles outside the door of the tower. They arrive in those mud-spattered motor-cars which can be seen in a country town on market-day or hurtling down a lane pulling trailers of milk-cans covered with pig netting. Or they come on powerful chromium-plated motor-bikes, on bicycles, or on foot. For the romantic, seeing his first band of ringers, they may be a disappointment, for none of them reach that collective ideal of a rustic which we all have in our minds, clinging always to the vision and not the fact. The younger

43

men will be wearing the clothes which their equivalent in the town would wear, and the older ones, with a more conventional rusticity, are wearing boots, their trousers neatly held in at the bottom with cycle-clips, and perhaps in summer a fat, highly perfumed rose for a button-hole. Ringing a bell, like croquet, requires more skill than strength, so physically the ringers are not all blacksmiths or champion sheaf pitchers; some are old and small.

When the captain arrives with the key to the tower, he will see if anyone is missing. If there is, they will all speculate as to where so-and-so could have got to. Perhaps the clergyman will come early to the church to prepare his service, and meet them there and make arrangements for ringing later in the week, a wedding on Tuesday or a funeral on Friday. Then, when they are all gathered outside the door, they stub out their cigarettes, take off their caps, and climb slowly up the stairs to the ringing chamber. There they sit down and rest, for they will have to stand for the next half-hour, and while they are resting they discuss which bell each shall ring. At last they stand up, take off their coats and roll up their sleeves. They lift the ropes off the hooks on the wall, coil up the ends into their left hands so that the ropes run under their thumbs and over their fingers, and raise their arms upwards and grip the furry sallies.

3

Ingenious Noted Ringers

THE ringers stand in a circle with their arms raised holding the sallies. The man ringing the treble bell, says "Treble, going, gone", and at the last word pulls on the rope, the others follow in the order of the bells. There are two ways of raising a ring in peal. The first is for the bells to sound in turn, the treble first, followed by the second up to the tenor. If numbers are used to represent their sound, this is what you will hear: 1, 1.12, 12.123, 123.1234, 1234.12345 and so on, striking in their order or in rounds till the bells are up. Quietly they sound at first, becoming louder as they swing through a greater arc at each successive swing. The other way, which is not widely practised outside Devon and Cornwall, is for the bells all to speak in order at the second or third sway, and when the treble starts to sound at handstroke, it is immediately behind the tenor. With numbers again used for sound: 123456; 123456; 1234561; 1234561;

12345612; 12345612; 123456123; 123456123; 1234561234;
1234561234; 12345612345; 12345612345; 123456123456;
and on in rounds striking very closely together till they are
up. This West Country method of raising in peal is extremely beautiful to hear, as the rhythm starting quickly
gets slower as the bells' swing increases, and is very different from the sound all too often heard when the bells are
raised singly, so that anyone listening on a Sunday morning, or before evensong, will hear each bell raised
separately, or two together, making a horrid ding-dong
noise.

When the bells are up and ringing rounds, it is possible
to judge the skill of each ringer. The real expert stands
with his feet close together, and carefully watches the man
who rings before him. Ringing is an endless succession of
arm bends above the head. The good ringer is rock-still
while doing these, the rope moving cleanly up and down,
a few inches from his face. The bad ringer bends his whole
body, and the rope makes great arcs and circles in the
air. The sallies fly up to the ceiling of the ringing chamber,
and sometimes, if this is very low, they will disappear
altogether at handstroke, darting down again like furry
caterpillars whose coily stripes are red, white, and blue,
or green and white and red; and with their movement the
tower shudders and twists with the force of the swinging
bells. Once up and ringing rounds, the treble ringer
will say "stand" at handstroke, and at the next
handstroke the bells are eased past their point of balance
and set. Perhaps a ringer will make a mistake and not set
his bell the first time, and ring by himself, becoming the
target for some shrewd piece of wit.

If you visit a church on a Sunday morning before the
service and meet the ringers outside the tower, after the
first few polite words you will be asked, "Are you a
ringer?" If the answer is "No", they become very helpful,
tell you exactly what they are doing and how they do it,
and after raising the bells they will take you up to the

belfry. There, in the dim light filtering through the louvres, the bells stand mouth upwards, green and dull. The clapper of each bell rests on one side of the sound bow, and on the other is a polished scar made by the iron wearing away the softer metal.

If you are not a ringer and get into a belfry by yourself and find the bells set, do not go near them, and touch nothing. If you walk about on the frame to get a closer look you may wobble, throw out a hand for support, and catch the wheel or the lip, the bell will turn over, and down you go to become a nasty mess of compound, comminuted fractures, squeezed between the frame and half a ton of copper and tin.

Every few years even an experienced ringer is killed or injured. Once when a ring had been left set, the band pulled off the bells in a peal, and then blood was seen running in a red coil down a rope. They found that a man had gone up to oil the gudgeons and been battered to death. In 1884, Edward Hart, a sawyer of Sturminster Marshall, near Wimborne in Dorset, rang in a wedding peal at Winterbourne Kingston; he became entangled in the rope, the bell lifted him up, cracked his head on the ceiling and then dropped him to the floor; he died soon afterwards. An Irishman was ringing for Mass at a chapel near Ballyhaunis, and the bell, which was hung in a tree, fell on his head and killed him. The Vicar of Barrington in 1885 was teaching some young ringers, when the rope coiled round his neck and lifted him off the floor, though luckily it did not hang him. By contrast, at Radcliffe-on-Trent in the same year, the bells were going well, when: "a tremendous noise was heard overhead, not indeed a 'Deep sound striking like a rising knell' but a rumble as if the whole seismic power contained in the bowels of the earth were concentrated up aloft and determined to vent its superabundant force in an effort to bring the tower, bells and all about the ears of the unfortunate ringers". The men rushed out of the tower, but when nothing more

47

happened they returned and found that one of the clappers had come off.

When the ringers leave you alone in the belfry to see the bells move, stand close to the door. A few muffled remarks from down below come faintly up the spiral staircase, and with a creaking of rope and wood, one bell turns over. Faster and faster it goes, till it has swung right round; just before it stops, the clapper, which is free, springs across the mouth and hits the soundbow, and the noise is metallic and harsh, not the clear note heard outside the church. After it come all the rest. The first few rounds are bearable; the wide mouths swing upwards and the stay fixed to the headstock circles to and fro, the white ropes snap over the ground pulley at backstroke, and the frame, if it is made of wood, can be seen moving. Then the noise becomes insupportable, the note of each bell merges into a singing dunce's cap of sound above one's head. Three or four minutes is as much as anyone can stand.

Ringing bells in rounds soon began to bore sixteenth-century ringers using the whole wheel. Once set, the bells could be pulled off in any order, say, on a ring of six bells, 1 3 5 2 4 6 instead of 1 2 3 4 5 6. Then it was found that the order in which the bells rang could be altered without setting them and starting again in a new order. If they were ringing rounds and the ringers wished the treble to change places with the second, the second was "cut down" or not allowed to swing through the complete circle, and it would strike sooner; and if the treble was "held off" or its swing increased slightly, the difference in time between the striking of the two bells would allow them to change places and the second strike in front of the treble. The order could be altered at handstroke or backstroke, and in "ringing changes", as this alteration of the order is called, the bells change every time they are rung at handstroke or backstroke.

Ringing changes in this way undoubtedly started soon after the invention of the whole wheel, for that allowed

48

the bells to be controlled, but its full implications were only beginning to be realised towards the end of the sixteenth century, and it was not till 1668 that Stedman published his *Tintinnalogia*. Stedman and other change ringers of this time were absorbed by the mystery and wonder of permutations. If you have two bells they can be rung in two different ways, 1 2 and 2 1; if you have three bells, in six; by writing down a ring of six bells in order from treble to tenor, 1 2 3 4 5 6, and then multiplying the figures together, it is possible to find the number of times the order can be altered without repetition—1 multiplied by 2 is 2, 2 multiplied by 3 is 6, 6 multiplied by 4 is 24, 24 multiplied by 5 is 120, and 120 multiplied by 6 is 720; so the order of six bells can be altered 720 times, and twelve bells 479,001,600 times. Mathematics of this kind naturally lead to such calculations as how long it would take a snail to climb Nelson's Column, or six million weeping widows to fill the North Sea with their salty tears.

Stedman's *Campanalogia* published in 1677 has a chapter on the "Art of Changes", giving three examples of this kind. If twelve bells were rung for their full extent of 479,001,600, at a rate of 720 an hour, though this is about twice the time it would take today, twelve men would have to ring for seventy-five years, twelve lunar months, one week, and three days. While if a man wrote the changes down on paper (the technical term for this is "pricking"), and put 1,440 on each sheet of paper, with 500 sheets to the ream, he would use 665 reams, which at five shillings the ream would cost £166 5s.

His second example is even more ingenious. He calculated that if the letters of the alphabet were used in every possible combination to form words of from two to twelve letters, they would produce the astounding number of 1,402,645,824,276,320 words, and if these were printed on large folio, 5,000 to a sheet, 561,058,329 reams of paper would be needed, and these could not be stored in all the houses of the City of London. At five shillings the ream, it would cost £140,564,582, or four times as much as the yearly rent of all the lands and houses of England, and the whole population of London, estimated at 500,000, reading 15,000 changes an hour, twelve hours a day, would be at their terrible task for forty years.

The last example he gives is one of those archetypes of arithmetic involving "A Man" or "A Boy" or "A Gardener"—in this case "A Man" and "A Brickmaker". A man with twenty horses goes to a rather simple brickmaker and says to him: "If I pay you one hundred pounds, will you let me take away as many bricks as a team of six horses can draw on a wagon, provided that no team of six horses is the same, and no team fetches more than one load." The brickmaker, not being a change ringer or a mathematician, agrees, and to his dismay finds that the man makes from his twenty horses 38,760 teams of six horses and no two teams alike. Each wagon takes five hundred bricks, so the brickmaker sees 19,380,000 bricks leaving his yard, costing the man a penny farthing a thousand. If the brickmaker is simple enough to allow the position of the horses in each team to be altered as well, 27,907,200 teams will carry off 13,953,600,000 bricks, which would build 93,024 houses, or six times the number destroyed in the Fire of London.

The last two chapters in Stedman's book describe the ways in which the order of the bells can be changed, by "plain changes" and "cross changes". In plain changes only two of the bells change at a time, so if there are six bells, 1 2 3 4 5 6, ringing rounds, on the first change the treble and second would change and the order would be 2 1 3 4 5 6; at the next change the treble would change with the third bell, and they would sound 2 3 1 4 5 6. In this way the treble moves from the lead till finally it changes places with the tenor, and the order is 2 3 4 5 6 1. This regular movement of a bell up and down is called "hunting", and is the basis of all change ringing. In plain changes, when the treble has reached the position of the tenor when they were ringing rounds it is said to "lie behind", and when it is there the two bells farthest from it change, so the order becomes 3 2 4 5 6 1. The treble now starts to "hunt down", the order for the next change being 3 2 4 5 1 6, and it will continue to move downwards till it is again in the lead. It is not necessary to start moving the treble when ringing plain changes, any of the other bells could start hunting up or down; nor is it necessary for the bells farthest from the hunting bell to change when it lies behind. But plain changes are hardly ever rung now, because the true change ringer wants ringing to be as complicated as possible.

Stedman's cross changes are the stock from which the involved ringing of today grew. The principle is that instead of changing one pair of bells, as many bells as possible are changed, so that if six bells ringing rounds go into changes, the first row would be 2 1 4 3 6 5 and the second 2 4 1 6 3 5 and the third 4 2 6 1 5 3. If the bells were altered in this way twelve times, they would be ringing rounds again, and would have only produced eleven of the possible 720 changes on six bells, so a "method" must be found to prevent the bells coming back into rounds, and it is the various methods of doing this which differentiate one set of changes from another. It would be tedious to go into all the methods used and the simplest means of preventing the bells coming back into rounds will suffice as an example. Six bells ringing cross changes as described by Stedman would after eleven changes be ringing in this order, 1 3 2 5 4 6; if the bell "ringing in second's place", or the position of the second bell in rounds, stays still, the bells behind it will be forced to move and the order will become 1 3 5 2 6 4. Now they can start to change as before, and the next alteration will produce 3 1 2 5 4 6, and on they go again. To distinguish one method from another they are given names.

In the *Campanalogia*, Stedman calls his methods of

ringing cross changes, Cross Peals, and the last part of the book is a collection of these on five, six, seven, and eight bells. He gives directions for ringing them. First he gives some peals for five bells, Phœnix, London Pleasure, Mr. Tendring's peal called Grand Paradox, What You Please, Reading Doubles, Grandsire; a first indication of the delights, pleasures, and paradoxes which are to come. Then there are fifty-three peals, composed by Fabian Stedman, with more sober names. On five bells there are Crambo, Primrose Orpheus, The Morning Star, The Quirister, The Faulcon, Merry Andrew, May Day, and St. Dunstan's Doubles; on six, A Cure For Melancholy, The Morning Exercise, The City Delight, London Nightingall, The Evening Delight, Non-such Bob, London Doubles, New Bob, and the Experiment; on seven, The Grand Experiment, and on eight, Wild Goose Chase. Then come Oxford peals with strange intimidating names— Adventure, Camelion, Medley, Fortune, Oxford Riddle or the Hermaphrodite, and My Lad. Last are the Cambridge peals. Stedman came from Cambridge and rang the bells of St. Benets, which with St. Botolph's sandwiches Corpus Christi. They are, My Honey, The Whirligige, Jack On Both Sides, Winwick Doubles, Non-such, Cambridge Delight and Cambridge Delight Another Way, The Dream, The Contention, The Cheat, Topsy-Turvie, The Parasite, The Tulip, Honeysuckle, Blunderbus, Hudibras, Jumping Doubles, Symphonie, The Antilope, The Maremaid, Checkquer, Marigold, Gogmagog, and another Nightingall. Stedman would have made a good nineteenth-century florist, he has the same sense of the liturgical and resonant. He would have admired a hyacinth called Og Roi de Basan, large white, pink eye; the dahlia Hero of Stonehenge; a rose called Village Maid, or two auriculas, Popplewell's Conqueror and Pollet's Ruler of England.

But change ringers today do not approve of all Stedman's cross changes, they have decided that no bell may move more than one place at a time, and that, except under certain conditions, no bell may strike more than two consecutive blows in the same place; a *peal* must be more than five thousand changes and anything less is a *touch*. In The Evening Delight, the second bell is in the lead for twenty consecutive changes, and this at once invalidates it, so that though of great interest these old peals are seldom heard today. If a new method is tried it will generally be more elaborate and involved than the one before, and the progression is always in this way, never backwards to the study of antiquity; although now that there is a strong feeling for a merry England of doublet, hose and artificial beard, a society of antiquarian ringers ' may arise for the practical exploration of their past.

There are also names to distinguish the number of bells rung in a method, and these are attached to the name of the method; five bells are called Doubles; six, Minor; seven, Triples; eight, Major; nine, Caters; ten, Royal; eleven, Cinques; and twelve, Maximus; so that if a method called Grandsire is rung on five bells, it is called Grandsire Doubles, and if on seven, Grandsire Triples. Today there are hundreds of methods, and they have all been collected ᴧnd published by the Central Council of Church Bell Ringers. In its *Collection of Minor Methods* it lists 177 ways of ringing six bells, which will produce a full extent of 720 changes. Although there are some names like Woodcock's Victory Bob, many of them have that improved nobility and gentry air : London Scholars Pleasure, Melandra Delight, Francis Genius Delight, Annable's London Surprise. They are all ideal for the conservatory or palm court, and all have a good heart, thick ivy leaves, or long glossy florets. But change ringing, born of the mathematical extravaganzas of the seventeenth century, must always produce this great maze of figures, made even more complicated by the fact that a method can be rung in many different ways. Besides the Central Council's collection of methods, it also issues collections of compositions, or the ways in which any method can be rung; for the method called Double Norwich Court Bob, it has collected 228 compositions of full peals. These are merely numbered and their composers only achieve immortality by having their names printed at the bottom of each, with the barest details of when and where it was first rung. Number 219 was first performed on Easter Monday, April 3rd, 1899, at St. John the Baptist's, Erith, by the Kent County Association, conducted by William Pye, composed by Edgar Wightman, and the 15,072 changes rung in nine hours twenty-four minutes.

One of the qualities which mark a legitimate method is regularity. If the movements of one bell through space and time are plotted on a graph so that its course, hunting up and down is a spiky zig-zag line, you will find in a regular method that there are some bits of the pattern which recur several times in different places; and if a complicated method is regular, it will be easier to ring than it looks, as the ringer finds large blocks of his work repeating themselves.

Music has no say in the eligibility of a method, though it may affect its popularity, and the composer will try and use the most musical changes which the method offers him to make up the 5,000 needed for a peal, marshalling his bobs and singles to bring the ten bells in Caters into the Tittums position, when the light and heavy bells strike alternately, or to avoid pairing the second with the Tenor in Major.

There is an opportunity to ring the old methods when a peal on five or six bells is attempted, for if six bells ring their full extent they will only produce 720 changes, and for a peal there must be more than 5,000. The ringers generally solve this problem by ringing 720 changes in one method seven times. In the eighteenth century seven different methods were sometimes rung to make up a peal; at Walsham-le-Willows in Suffolk in 1760, a peal was rung on six bells using London Surprise, Cambridge Surprise,

Francis' Genius, Francis' Goodwill, Oxford Treble Bob, Court Bob, and Grandsire Bob, and twenty-eight years later the ringers of Halstow at Hoo rang forty-two different five-bell methods to make a peal of 5,040 changes in three hours eighteen minutes. Today if complete extents —or 720's—in different methods are too easy for a peal on six bells, two or more methods can be spliced together into extents of 720 changes, to make the ringing even more complicated and enable the ringers to ring more than seven methods in the seven extents which form their peal.

The change ringer must be able to ring his bell so easily that he can concentrate entirely on the movement of the others through their intricate course. The technique is known as "Ropesight"; he looks at the other ropes to see who is ringing in front and behind him, and by a series of mnemonics knows what he should do at any time. But sometimes in a tower where the ringers are not particularly skilled or when new ringers are being trained, there will be charts hanging on the wall of the ringing chamber with the course of the bells marked in coloured chalk. These are despised by the puritans, who feel that anyone should be able to remember the work of the bell he is ringing. Ever since Stedman, there have been books on how to ring bells and how to ring methods. Jasper Snowdon was the great late nineteenth-century expert, and all his books are still being reprinted and make the best introduction to anyone wishing to study ringing, ropesight, and changes. But the most monumental work of all is Shipway's *Campanalogia*, published in 1816; and for this century there are the books of J. Armiger Trollope, and the collections of peals and methods published by the Central Council of Church Bell Ringers.

When a band has successfully rung a peal, it will put a board or a tablet, or paint on the wall of the belfry the peal, the time it took, the date, and the names of the ringers. The earliest of these are in Norwich, one commemorating the first peal of 5,040 changes ever rung, in 1715, and the second the first peal of Grandsire Triples, at the church of St. Peter Mancroft. The board is this shape ⌐⌒⌐. There are inverted bells on the apex of the semicircle and the top corners of the rectangle, replacing the storied urns which would be there if this was a sepulchral monument; they are inscribed with stock phrases, "Now let all contention cease", "We must own truth", and "Deserves place". In the semicircular part, two podgy angels wave palm branches over another bell surmounted by a crown, and from their knees fall well-starched scrolls, bearing the words "Love as Brethren". On the rectangular part of the board is this inscription:

"On the 26th of August 1718 was rung that harmonious peal called Grandsire Triples which have been the study of the most ingenious men of this age who delight in the art of variation, but all their projections have proved errors until it was undertook by John Garthon who with long study and practice have perfectly discovered those intricate methods which were hidden from the eyes of all the ringers in England, the extent of this peal being 5,040 changes have often been rung with changes alike, but the first time that it was rung true was in three hours and a half without any changes alike, or a bell out of course, by these men, whose names are under written against their bells as they rung."

James Brooke	Treble	Henry Howard	5
John Briggs	2	Wm. Callow	6
Wm. Palmer	3	Tho. Melchior	7
Robt. Crane	4	Tho. Barrett	Tenor

Nowadays peal-boards are not so elaborate or so informative, only recording the ringers, the peal, the time, and the rector and churchwardens. Angels no longer hold up bells, and the tablet is often pedimented and inscribed with that special ecclesiological signwriting evolved during the first part of this century, the letters sprouting into spikes, fleurs-de-lys and crosses.

After these first peals of true changes, ringers concentrated on different methods, but at Leeds in Kent, in 1761. 40,320 changes were rung in twenty-seven hours. But this does not count as a true record, although no one has exceeded it, because relays of ringers rang the bells, but 21,600 changes of Bristol Surprise Major were rung in twelve hours fifty-eight minutes in 1950 at Over in Cheshire.

If a band gets bored with the old round of peals in different methods, they can make them eccentric in a number of ways. One man will attempt to ring two bells, or the whole band will be ex-Service men of the same regiment, or policemen, or clergymen, or brothers of the Ancient Order of Free Foresters, or Masons, or brothers and fathers, or all brothers, or all have the same Christian name—a Frederick's or Charles's peal. Sometimes they will increase the technical difficulties, by not having a conductor to call "Bob" or "Single", and the other incantations. Sometimes they will all be over a certain age—an octogenarians' peal, a peal rung by adolescents; or of the same trade—a bellfounders' peal, a bakers' peal. Since Mrs. Alice White broke a record by being the first woman to ring in a tower bell peal in 1912, the lust for variation can be gratified by even more combinations—aunts and uncles, brothers and sisters, mothers and daughters; and two ringers will celebrate their engagement with a peal of Spliced Surprise. If peals become too much, they can ring a Date Touch which in 1967 would be 1967 changes.

There was a typical gathering at Powderham Church, which stands on the west bank of the River Exe, when six men and women met to attempt a peal of Cambridge Minor. They left their cars and motor-cycles on a wide verge of dank brown earth under a clump of yews, and walked up to the west door of the church, where they were welcomed by the vicar and the captain of the local ringers. The inside of the church was decorated for Easter. Clumps of primroses stood in moss round the base of the font, and trails of ivy hung from the reading-desks; the pillars and arches were white, and the walls soft red sandstone, eroded like the cliffs which rise above the railway running along the seashore between Dawlish and Teignmouth.

At some time in the last half of the last century the ropes from the bells were brought down into the body of the church; a hoop of iron with wooden guides set into its circumference prevents the ropes moving too much in their long drop from the ceiling to the floor. One of the ropes had been spliced where it was rubbed away by its guide, and another rope was fitted to the bell in case the old one should break in the middle of the peal. When they decided which bells they were to ring, the bells were rung up and set. Then they saw that the ropes lay comfortably in their hands, and one very tall man tied up the tail of his with a strong piece of whipcord, because it was too long for him. Lastly they made their final preparations, rolling up sleeves and loosening ties, making sure that belts were tight. Then this prayer was said: "Lord, when Thou givest to Thy servants grace to undertake any great matter; grant us to know that it is not the beginning, but the continuing thereof until it be thoroughly finished, that yieldeth the true glory; through Him who for the finishing of Thy work died for us, even Jesus Christ our Lord." The bells were pulled off in rounds, the conductor on one handstroke said "Go Cambridge", and at the next handstroke they went into changes. The familiar sound of the bells running down the scale gave place to the ordered confusion of the method, bim bom ting pega bega bome, bom bim pega ting bome bega, on into the first extent of 720 changes. Occasionally the conductor called out his instructions or put an erring ringer back in his proper place. After a quarter of an hour they looked like runners just before they get their second wind; some were beginning to breathe more heavily, others were well into their stride, perhaps a little paler and darker round the eyes, but perfectly capable of ringing for another two and a quarter hours. Their eyes darted from side to side as they looked to see who was ringing before and behind them, the ropes moved through the guides with a chatter like the conversation of gargoyles, and the sound of the bells came faintly down through the tower. The first 720 changes were rung in twenty-one minutes.

After listening and watching inside the church, one wants to go outside, listen to the bells, and goggle gloomily at the landscape. Powderham is ideally sited for this. On the west a ridge of hills rises in even slopes of pale green and red, crowned with a triangular belvedere tower built in 1773. To the east the road bends round the churchyard, and a culvert, filled with the junk of a tidal river—sea-weed, old tennis-shoes, and paper bags—goes under the railway to the muddy beach. Across the wide river are more hills and tall pine trees rising behind "À la Ronde" —that monument to leisure—and still farther away, Exmouth, lit by flat spring sunshine, like a marine view of the 1820s. Two trains passed, one going fast to London with a fireman who waved, and another to Torquay with a beautiful green engine driven by a man in the cleanest pale blue overalls, standing morosely on his footplate. Just after he had gone by, something went wrong, the bells ran together with a horrid jangling and stopped; one rang four more times before it too stopped. Inside the church the ringers looked unhappy, for their peal was spoilt by an accident and not by any fault of theirs. The string used to tie up the long tail of the tall man's rope had broken so that it flapped about in his face; he had lost himself and the peal was marred.

The one great fault in change ringing is that a ringer cannot help feeling like a worm if there is an accident caused by some mistake (which he might make at the last change in a peal), and the more sympathetic the others are the worse it is. However, after a rest they decided that though there was not time to ring a peal, they would try a quarter peal of 1,260 changes, which was successful; and so they were able to go home satisfied.

The oldest surviving society of bell ringers is the Ancient Society of College Youths. Since their foundation in 1637 members of this society have been consistently active in change ringing in all parts of the country; they ring at St. Paul's Cathedral.

In the 1660s, Richard Palmer was the leader of a distinguished band of ringers at Bedford, and in the Bodleian Library at Oxford there is a manuscript book with the changes he invented written down with Greek and Hebrew numbers instead of Arabic, and also his settings of the psalms to be played on church bells. The first part of this book is a series of conceited epigrams on his skill written by his admirers, with such charming lines as these:

> . . . for I believe
> Your mother [Palmer] when she did conceive
> Your noble selfe, imagin'd she did heare
> A rare melodious Peal ring in ye air
> And it had been but just for music then
> To present ye Prologue of your life; when
> Each act thereof is stored with such sweet delightful tunes.

Two more couplets show the style of the rest:

> England's ye ringing Isle, may I divine
> Palmer's the second Englands—Palmerine,

and:

> Yet thought I had o' th' Royall Company
> Whose leader is Grave Remla Previlo.

The last two words are heavily marked with a rather blotted asterisk and explained—"Oliver Palmer Backward".

Many other societies were formed in the seventeenth and eighteenth centuries with such names as the Western

Green Caps, The Croydon Youths, the Leeds Youths and Lenham Society, and the Norwich Scholars, who from 1727 to 1844 were the most inventive and skilled ringers. One of the great attractions of ringing then was that it was considered good physical exercise, and for a time became fashionable; accounts and histories always emphasise the aristocratic members of these societies. At Knole between 1603 and 1608 a machine was installed so that devotees of this craze could perform the movements of ringing a bell without making any noise. In an attic there was a roller supported above the floor, and from it radiated four iron rods with a heavy lead weight fixed to the end of each, a rope was wound round the roller and dropped through the floor into a room below. When the rope was pulled, the weights spun round, rolling the rope up again on to the roller so that they could be pulled first one way and then the other. There was a similar machine at New College, Oxford; and Addison and Benjamin Franklin exercised themselves on dumb-bells of this kind installed in their bedrooms.

Many of these early societies collapsed through lack of interest, and one of these, the Rambling Club of Ringers, was active in London from 1733 to 1735; a man called Laughton recorded their visits to various towers. Parts of his account are in doggerel, always popular with ringers, from the first crude rules written in church towers to poems describing the work of bells in different methods which appear in the *Ringing World* still. Today besides the College Youths, there are the Royal Cumberland Youths, who were named in honour of the Duke of Cumberland; they also ring in London and have a membership scattered all over Great Britain, the Dominions, and Colonies.

All the greatest ringers have belonged to one or other of these ringing societies, and are commemorated in the histories and at annual dinners. The College Youths toast their masters of three, two, and one hundred years ago, so with the passing of time all will be remembered. But perhaps the ringer who was most renowned was Dr. Samuel Lee; as a young man he was a friend of Samuel Lawrence, one of the heaviest men in England, who weighed thirty-two stone and who rang many peals in the Midlands. Lee was a carpenter, and when he could read and write, bought himself a copy of Ruddiman's Grammar and taught himself Latin. His system was to memorise a book, then sell it and buy another; before he was twenty-five he knew Latin, Greek, and Hebrew, and had started to learn Chaldee, Syriac, Samaritan, Persian, and Hindustani. Then he had the good fortune to lose his carpentering tools, and started to earn a living by teaching at Bowdler's Foundation School at Shrewsbury, till he was sent to Cambridge by the Church Missionary Society in 1813. He took his degree as Doctor of Divinity in 1833, and became first, Professor of Arabic and then Regius Professor of Hebrew. Before his death in 1852 he had translated parts of the Bible into Hindustani, Persian, Arabic, and Coptic, and published a number of sermons and pamphlets.

Few other ringers have achieved the eminence of Samuel Lee, though many were famous in the small circle of their society or county. Some have memorials in the church whose bells they rang—brass tablets, candlesticks for the altar, their names on the bells, or stained-glass windows of angels, scrolls, and heavenly orchestras of shawm, sackbut, and virginals. One of the best epitaphs for a ringer is in St. Giles, Norwich; on the wall of the belfry there is a slab inscribed with these six lines:

Near to this place John Webster fell,
Beloved by all who knew him well.
The most ingenious noted ringer,
St. Giles sixth bell round did bring her,
He closed the peal, struck well his bell,
Ceasing the same down dead he fell.
> *November 17th, 1760, in the 63rd year of his age.*

Until 1891 the ringing societies and Guilds had no

central organisation, but in that year Sir Arthur Heywood founded the Central Council of Church Bell Ringers.

The Council consists of representatives of the Associations and Guilds, and meets once a year to discuss the welfare of change ringing. One of its first acts was to lay down the rules defining a method and to start the collections of peals and compositions which it has since published. In 1901 the Council issued a glossary of technical terms, and later, model rules for ringers and hints on the maintenance of church bells and towers.

The Council is extremely strict in the interpretation of what constitutes true change ringing, and is apt at times to overlook questions involving æsthetics, preferring to solve them dogmatically rather than by intuition or taste. Once it was suggested that when a half-muffled peal was rung it would sound more beautiful and moving if each change was repeated, first with the bell sounding with its full strength and then with the blow of the clapper dulled by the pad strapped on to one side; but no two changes must be repeated, and so an excellent idea is not officially approved despite the fact that ringers will continue to do this. The Associations and Guilds (other than the two societies, the College Youths and the Cumberland Youths, who send delegates to its meetings) cover all parts of England and Wales. More often than not if the area represented is a Diocese, the organisation will be called a Guild, and if merely a County it will be an Association.

Like other minorities in this country, the ringers have their own weekly newspaper. The *Bell News and Ringing Record* was published in weekly parts from February 1881 to December 1915, and the *Ringing World* from March 1911 to the present day, still appearing every Friday. The issues of *Bell News* for the last twenty years of the nineteenth century are so completely of their time that any copy will evoke a sepia photograph of the period. Besides the large half-page advertisements for the different bell foundries, there are such delights as the Paragon,

Antelope, and Flying Scud, front and rear steering, ball-bearing, double-driving tricycles; and the Mazeppa all-steel bicycle, ideal for ringing excursions. Change-ringing gardeners advertised in the "Situations and Wanted" column; one continued to look for a new job throughout 1902. Other change ringers who were in the photography business, asked for Cartes-de-visite and Cabinets to be sent to them for enlargement. Gillett and Johnston, the great Croydon founders, had a nice cut of Old Father Time zooming round a church tower, and another founder a huge bell for "church, ship, fog, school, and factory". There were splendid suit lengths of black and blue serges and vicunas at twenty-one shillings each, and music to be played on handbells—"Norah, the Pride of Kildare" and "The Swiss Toy Girl".

Most of the paper was taken up with reports of association meetings, successful peals, new compositions, short histories of ringers and churches, and a fine fiery correspondence column testy with such phrases as "Heartily sick of these questions" and "It is obvious to the merest tyro". In the summer long columns would describe the outings of the various bands and societies.

The annual outing is still a great event in the year, ranging from the village ringers, who take their wives and their girl or boy friends on a tour of towers, when they ring a touch at one and then go on to another, finishing perhaps with a large tea at the seaside, to the highly efficient tours of large associations and devoted peal ringers who will spend a week ringing in a county. Either they arrange at each village that they shall ring there, or they "Tower grab", arriving without any notice and asking the clergyman if they may ring his bells. In 1885 the St. Peter's Society of Sheffield had their annual outing to Liverpool, where before lunch they rang a peal, and then went to New Brighton. Here some members of the party occupied themselves with photography, while some found "an abundance of charming young ladies soliciting orders for

refreshment in quite a novel manner". But the beau-ideal
of a ringing tour must always be a Bank Holiday visit of
some Cumberland Youths to the Isle of Thanet.

They assembled on the platform at the terminus of the
London Chatham and Dover Railway, wearing coats done
up by the top button, and those boaters which were
speckled like the soft feathers of Spangled Hamburghs or
Silver Polish hens. At last the reserved coach drew up,
and the party, carefully listed as Mister or Esquire, like
professional and amateur cricketers, climbed into the
carriage. During the journey they whiled away the time
with touches on handbells, in friendly chats, or admiring
the corn and hops growing beside the line. When they
arrived at their inn in Birchington, they sat straight down
to a knife-and-fork tea, and Mr. John Mansfield, "officiat-
ing for the nonce as Cumberland's Jester, kept the risible
faculties of the guests in constant exercise, and the coy
young damsel who ministered to their wants, after vain
attempts to keep her countenance, was obliged to join in
the general hilarity". After tea they rang their handbells
and played old English games, until Captain Thomas sent
his party to Bedfordshire.

Next morning was Sunday and they had breakfast at
six, when the chairman and vice did a brisk business
amongst ham, eggs, coffee, etc.; a few of them bathed,
others were content with a sniff of the briny ocean. Then
they walked along the dusty lanes and into the fields on
the way to Quex Tower, disturbing on the way the "usual
biped and quadruped creatures found in such beautifully
wooded demesnes". After a peal, a pair of wagonettes took
them for the semi-marine drive to Margate, and when they
had rung some touches on the bells of St. John's, they
went to the pier "where would be found all the fashionables
and exquisites of the place, we might say that it was the
attractiveness of one or two specimens of the human form
so artistically decorated that caused two of the juvenile
members of the party to fail meeting at the rendezvous,

and who had in consequence to walk home": a great opportunity for Mr. Mansfield. On Monday morning before breakfast in the first light of dawn, the Cumberlands were tumbling about in the sea like so many young porpoises, while others rang handbells on the beach. This was the last day of their holiday, they did not do much ringing, and when they espied a house of entertainment called the Powell Arms, they went in "and the jester again to the fore kept them all alive by his irresistible fun". That evening a train took the party back to London, and as it travelled on the long viaduct above the blue and violet fields of slate, they agreed with their jester when he said, "Back in Old England again".

The *Ringing World* competed with *Bell News* for four years. From the very beginning it was a much smarter paper; there was a competition for the person who succeeded in making the largest number of new subscribers (a set of handbells was the prize), and in the summer of 1911 it organised a vast Gala Ringers' Day at the Festival of Empire held in the Crystal Palace. The advertisements lost their Victorian quality because new advertisers made new blocks for the new paper; but one picture of three very pretty ink-wells in the shape of bells appeared in the *Ringing World* for nearly thirty years. The typography and paper were also better, though, perhaps to build a tradition, the format has only been slightly altered in forty years. Now it is the official journal of the Central Council, and its leading articles show the change in ringing during the last hundred years. These are often concerned with the spiritual welfare of the ringers, asking them if they are true servants of the Church, and encouraging that self-analysis which seeks to drive out complacency and slackness. This paper is the mirror of change ringing, but it seldom notices the activities of a minority who practise a different art—the call-change ringers.

In some belfries there are large boards with the changes

of a method written down and numbered on the left-hand side; call-change ringers do not remember the way the bells move at each change, but refer to the board. After ringing rounds, the conductor calls out "One", and if the method was Grandsire Doubles, the order would change to 2 1 3 5 4. They will ring in this order for as long as the conductor wishes, and then he will call "Two" and they make the next change, which is to 2 3 1 4 5. Another system is to call out the numbers of the bells which are to change places, "Two to three" or "Four to five" and in this way ring plain changes. The confirmed change ringer, or "method ringer", or "follower of the Exercise" is apt to criticise this simple ringing, and refer to it as "Grindstone Bob" or "Churchyard Bob", and describe call-change competitions as "Miserable jousts", "Contemptible displays", or "Pitiful Money Scrambles"; and when a competent musician makes a criticism that the æsthetics of bell ringing depend too much on mathematics and too little on music, they say this is true of call changes but not of method ringing. However, these criticisms are in part justified, for a method ringer is more versatile and will be able to ring any bell in a ring, while the call-change ringer usually only rings one particular bell. Certainly, once a call-change ringer has learnt to ring methods, he finds it more entertaining and seldom wishes to return to call changes. Call-change ringers, though, excel at raising and lowering bells in peal and in the rhythm of their striking, and even if their music may become monotonous, when a good call-change band is ringing in its own tower, where each man knows the idiosyncrasies of his own bell, the crisp precision of the striking is a sublime sound. There is, of course, one great disadvantage to this intense specialisation of one man being able only to ring one bell with real skill; if a member of the band leaves the parish or dies, or is ill, there is no one to replace him immediately and a skilful successor may take some time to train.

Devonshire and Cornwall are the counties where call

changes are most popular, and in the summer they have competitions, when towers in all parts of the county compete against each other. In Cornwall the prize is money to be divided between each member of the band most successful in raising the bells, ringing *rounds,* and falling in peal. Devonshire call-change ringers have to ring for fifteen minutes and raise and fall in peal, but instead of ringing rounds they ring call changes. Every Saturday in Devonshire there will be a competition, perhaps for a cup given by a parishioner and competed for in his parish, but the premier events are those organised by the Devon Association of Ringers.

The Association's North Devon Six Bell Competition for 1953 was held at Halberton, a village a few miles to the east of Tiverton where, as well as the competition, there seems to be a peculiar and beautiful strain of geranium, which can be seen in many of the windows on the main street, pink with deep violet blotches. The church is away from the main road, and may be reached in two ways, one down a narrow road past a picturesque pond, and the other, is a wider road which ends in a cul-de-sac. A path runs between the church and the school and turns round the churchyard. Cars and buses filled the cul-de-sac and lined the nearby roads, and the ringers walked up to the church for the service which, by the Rules of the Association, must start each competition.

Nothing more clearly shows the change which has come upon ringing in the last hundred years than this—today, ringers are humble church workers, no longer tag-rags. The service began with a hymn, played with a good solid Ancient and Modern rhythm, then the Lord's Prayer was said and the 122nd and 150th Psalms sung, and, after the Creed, Responses, and Confession, the Association's own Prayer.

"Grant, O Lord, that whosoever shall be called by the sound of the Bells to Thy House of Prayer, may enter into

Thy Gates with thanksgiving, and unto Thy Courts with praise.

"And we beseech Thee, O Heavenly Father, to pour Thy Grace into the hearts of all Ringers, who everywhere engage in the art of bellringing for Thy Service.

"Bless us, O Lord, with skill and endurance whilst ringing, so that the music of our Bells shall delight the ear of all Thy people, and call them to worship Thee in the beauty of Holiness.

"Endow us, O Lord, with the virtues of punctuality, patience and good comradeship, but, above all 'reverence, that we may at all times ring only to Thy Honour and Glory.

"Amen."

Before the Blessing and the National Anthem, the ringers sing a special hymn, richly symbolic, as this verse shows:

Then go! Ye ringers good,
Your Captain now obey,
His lead if understood
Will guide each perfect sway.
Thus more and more
With ear and sight
And art and might
His Name adore.

After this short service, the judges went into the school to the room where they were to stay for the rest of the afternoon; they must not know who is ringing, but decide entirely on what they hear. Meanwhile, the secretary of the Association, after many cries of "Order" to stop the burr of conversation, called out the names of the villages competing. "St. Giles in the Wood," he cried, and the captain of the band came up to the church gate, and reached up to a grey felt hat, held head high, and drew out a number, nine. Each captain drew in the same way, Down St. Mary, Rackenford, Rewe, and the rest. Then the teams which had drawn numbers one and two went into the church, and the door was shut behind them, and when once inside they drew lots again to decide who should ring first. Throughout the afternoon the teams went in two by two.

The three judges sat on red folding chairs round a yellow table in the bare class-room dedicated to them. Each had a notebook to mark down his score, and they waited there, discussing past ringers and the day's form till the treble bell chimed three times as a signal that the first team was about to start. Then the bells spoke, and one judge checked the time to make sure that they did not ring for less than a quarter of an hour. Their lips moved slightly as they counted quickly 1 2 3 4 5 6, 1 2 3 4 5 6, 1 2 3 4 5 6, seeing that no bell missed a stroke and that they struck with the same interval between each. The score is marked in whole, half, and quarter faults, written down in the notebooks. When the first team had lowered the bells in peal and finished, the points were added up, and the scores of the judges averaged to give the final figure. Like cross-country running, a call-change competition is one of those sports in which the fewer points the better the score.

Throughout the afternoon the ringers stood leaning on the iron railing outside the churchyard. Alternately listening and talking—when a poor team rang they paid no attention, only wincing at a particularly bad bit of ringing; but when the favourites rang, they looked up at the tower or down on the ground, noticing every slight alteration of rhythm and pace. Ringing competitions are one of the pleasantest forms of rural festivity; the rumble of conversation is like a market-day or race-meeting, and the colours are the same too, the pale greys and buffs of soft mackintoshes shimmering amongst the stiff blue and brown suitings. Cups of tea were on sale at the school and the public house had an extension till four o'clock. All the time the bells rose, rang, and fell, while the critics leant on the polished iron rail, perhaps putting a hand over an ear to still the sound of the bells while they listened to some piece of gossip from another member of the "Lovely brotherhood", as they call their membership of a band of ringers.

At four o'clock there was a tea interval for three-quarters of an hour. In the two remaining class-rooms of the school, whose walls were hung with the flotsam of contemporary education—portraits of the Royal Family cut from illustrated papers; a map of the world with paper ribbons joining stamps stuck round its edges to their countries; daring infantile abstract paintings, crayon drawings of galleons; rabbits' skulls and the debris from an owl's nest pinned to a sheet of white paper; potted-meat pots with auriculas and pansies; Millais' "The Boyhood of Raleigh"; school books draped beneath a Union Jack; and Our Breakfast Table, packets of patent foods, and tea, coffee, and cocoa labels gummed to a sheet of black paper —stood trestle tables covered with white cloths. Among the piled plates of pasties, egg and lettuce sandwiches, tomato and cheese sandwiches, scones split and covered with cream and jam, sausage rolls, sponge cakes and cream buns were flowers, lilies of the valley and vast dark red parrot tulips, destroying the bitter smell of chalk and ink. Such a tea as this would only displease one person, the late J. H. Kellogg, M.D., author of *Plain Facts,* who considered tea the most inflaming of all meals.[1]

After the tea interval the ringing started again, till at a quarter-past six, one team alone was left, the favourites, St. Giles-in-the-Wood. Everyone was silent after the warning bell had struck, and as they waited tensely for the first sound of all the bells ringing up, a dark cloud blotted out the watery sun, turning the red sandstone tower the colour of dried blood. Midges bobbed about among the yew trees, and at last the bells spoke. Quickly at first, then slower as they were raised till they rang rounds with an easy turning rhythm, on into changes and back to rounds

---

[1] If your public library has no copy of this American masterpiece, here is the relevant passage; the author is discussing the temptations which a clergyman meets in life. "When the minister goes out to tea, he is served with the richest cake, the choicest jellies, the most pungent sauces, and the finest of fine-flour bread-stuffs. Little does the indulgent hostess dream that she is ministering to the inflammation of passions which may imperil the virtue of her own daughter, or even her own. Salacity once aroused, even in a minister, allows no room for reason or for conscience."

71

again, the hum note of each bell combined in one throbbing note. At the end of fifteen minutes they were lowered. This is the tensest time, for after the bells are down and are silent once again, one may swing too far and strike once more. But St. Giles-in-the-Wood made no fault, and the competition finished.

Little girls had been walking about with penny notebooks during the afternoon, collecting money for a raffle, and before the five certificates which were the prizes for the competition were presented at the church door, yet another draw was made. A table covered with green baize was placed across the church porch, and on the ground in front of it in a wooden box, wrapped in red, white, and blue paper, was the prize for the raffle—a chicken dinner, one dressed rooster, one large cauliflower, a bunch of parsley, two leeks, and some potatoes; the second prize was a mysterious flat, brown paper parcel; and the third was twenty cigarettes.

After the draw there were cries of "Order", and the chairman of the Association made a short speech, thanking the ladies who prepared the tea, and the rector for allowing them to use his tower, and then he read out the marks scored by each team. First was St. Giles-in-the-Wood with sixteen points, and the captain of the band walked up to the porch and was given the first certificate. This is elaborately printed with the name of the Association and the competition, in gold and red and green, and at the bottom, within a printed border, is a photograph of Halberton Church. It now hangs in the ringing chamber at St. Giles, beside all the others which this parish has won. Second came West Down with eighteen points, and third Down St. Mary with twenty-three, fourth Chawleigh, and fifth Mortehoe. Each of these teams was given a certificate, and then the names of the remainder were read out in order of merit—Swimbridge, Rose Ash, Rackenford, Rewe, and Bishops Nympton. That was the end of the North Devon Six Bell Competition for that year.

This intense activity of change ringers and call-change ringers is the basis of that ringing which we hear on Sundays and on the Feasts of the Church. At other times one may be disturbed by a peal attempt or a competition, but this minority, which so audibly asserts itself, is a peaceful one. Sometimes one of the 50,000 ringers in this country will be bobbery and unpleasant, not because he is a ringer but because he is made that way. If ever you live close to a bell tower and have good reason to object to three hours' ringing on a hot summer's afternoon when you are sick in bed with the wilts, ask them to stop and they will, lowering their bells, perhaps singly or perhaps in peal; but willing to cease for your comfort, and leaving the ropes, hooked up to the wall of the ringing chamber, but still rising and falling slightly with the dying movement of each bell.

4

Ringing for Special Occasions

THIS century there are few occasions which encourage us to put on peculiar clothes, dance in the
streets, or eat special foods. We seem to have confined our joy to four festivals, three of them religious and
one secular, to the yearly holiday, to organised games on
Saturday afternoons—a tradition of docility founded in
the school yard—and to quiet Sundays. There are, though,
the movable feasts of clubs, societies, and associations;
their charabancs, no longer called "The Fruits of Peace"
or "Heart of Midlothian", no longer with key-bugles and

74

the canvas top furled at the back, but still roaring up and down the country to visit scenes of natural beauty, coming from the mining villages and market-towns, out against the flow of those seeking a new picturesque, which they find in the deserted cindery streets, winding gear, and chimneys. Previously, people found their amusements in their own community or within the radius of a day's walk; some of these entertainments were religious, some were secular, some were not pleasurable at all, and for most of them the church bells rang. Many, however, succumbed from a variety of causes; the death of the last man to preserve a tradition, or from sloth, or Puritanism, or the Reformation, or education. In places where they are kept up they are a trifle selfconscious, like the Hawaiian goose, while others flourish on the publicity given to them by the newspapers.

Before the laity's special ringing the church's must be described. The church provided the bells in its tower so that the congregation could be reminded of its festivals and services. When a priest was being inducted into his new parish, he would ring one bell to let his parishioners know that he was there, the number of strokes was supposed to represent the number of years he would spend in the living. Before the Reformation the Sanctus bell, which still hangs in some churches, was rung during the Mass; three times at the Sanctus, once before the Elevation, three times at the Elevation of the Host, three times at the Elevation of the Chalice, once at the Elevation before the Pater, and three times at the Domine, non sum Dignus, and also when the Sacrament was being carried to the sick. Today Roman Catholics in this country use little bells like bicycle-bells, which can be rung by shaking them or by some ingenious mechanism. The Sanctus bell became known as the Ting Tang for its sound, or as a Dagtale bell, which might be a corruption of Day-counting bell, rung to show the day of the month, in the same way that Great St. Mary's in Cambridge rings the day of the month every

75

night at nine o'clock. At Frodsham Church in Cheshire the Dagtale bell hung outside the tower, and on feast days, when the bells stopped ringing before the service, a man would lean out, and when he saw the vicar approaching he would ring the bell.

In some parishes a Sacrament bell was rung before the Communion Service; this would be a different one from the Ting Tang, so that there could be no confusion between the two. Another special bell would be the Sermon bell, rung to tell people that a sermon would be preached at that service. In the seventeenth century, after prayers were said, the Sermon bell would ring so that Dissenters would come into the church and listen to the sermon. The Tantony bell, a corruption of St. Anthony, who had a bell attached to the head of his staff or round the neck of his pig, summoned the priest to the church. But the most famous of all these is the bell of "Bell, Book, and Candle". The Prayer of Excommunication or Anathema was read before an assembly of priests, holding tall wax candles in their hands; immediately after the prayer, they cast these candles to the floor, the book was closed, and a bell rung.

As well as these bells which regulate the parish, the priest, and the services, the events in life which touch the church are also commemorated with the ringing of bells. When the Banns of Marriage were read for the first time and no one had risen to their feet to say that the spinster and bachelor should not be joined together in Holy Matrimony, a Banns Peal or Spurring Peal was rung at Beckingham and Saundby in Nottinghamshire. After the wedding service, a peal would be rung for the bride and groom; and in Hertfordshire, if a rope broke, it was a superstition that the marriage would turn out to be unlucky. At Strouton in Lincolnshire the church had only one bell, so that for weddings three men would climb into the belfry and strike the bell with hammers to make it sound like a ring. At Treswell in Nottinghamshire the whole party climbed upstairs to the belfry after the wedding service, and the best man gave a large loaf of currant bread and a cheese to the oldest ringer, who shared it out amongst the school children. Then the bells rang for the rest of the day; and on the morning after, as was common in other parts of England before honeymoons became the rule, they rang a Bride's Peal to wake up the happy or disillusioned pair, whose initials were then written up in the belfry with the date of the marriage. In many places when children were baptised, the bells rang for a short time after the service, and unbaptised children who died from the numerous diseases which made infancy so perilous were buried without a single bell sounding for them. Confirmation was also a time for ringing, but the peal was more in honour of the bishop than of the girls and boys. Not till one was dying were the bells really used to their full and most lugubrious effect.

The Sixty-seventh Canon of the Church of England orders, "That when any is passing out of this life, a bell shall be tolled, and then the minister shall not then be slack to do his last duty", and the Articles of Visitation of the Diocese of Worcester for 1667 ordered that a passing bell should be rung in order that the living should think of their own deaths, and that they might "commend the other's weak condition to the mercy of God". The passing bell was one of the first of these special tollings to be silenced; perhaps through sloth on the part of the clergy who would not disturb themselves to perform their last duty; perhaps the sextons found it too cold a job in winter, and were not as fortunate as Scarlett, the sexton of Peterborough, who in 1572 was given "a gowne beyng a poore olde man and rysng oft in the nyghts to tolle ye bell for sicke persons, ye wether beynge grevous". At the beginning of the eighteenth century it was customary to toll only after death, and this was called a Death Knell, or a Soul Bell, to encourage the parish to pray for the dead. There were many ways of ringing this knell—the bell might be tolled for a long time, and then the age of the

man or woman struck out slowly; different bells were sometimes rung for men and women; the renowned Nine
Tailors or tellers', nine-strokes struck for a man; or three
tolls for a man and two for a woman. At Marsham in
Suffolk they were known as Knocks for the Dead, three
knocks for a girl, four for a boy, six for a spinster, seven
for a matron, eight for a bachelor, and nine for a husband.

After death there was more ringing—a winding peal,
when the corpse was laid out and put into its shroud. The
soul was not supposed to leave the body after burial till
a bell had been rung, which also drove away evil spirits.
The Puritans disliked burial peals, and objected to such
ringing as marked the death of Lady Isabella Berkeley in
1516, when "There was ringing daily, that is to say at St.
Michael's 33 peals, at Trinity 33 peals, at St. John's 33,
at Babylake because it was so nigh 57 peals and in the
Mother Church 30 peals and every peal twelve pence".
Today it is usual for there to be a muffled peal, or the
tolling of one bell; and at the funeral of ringers a touch
on handbells is sometimes rung over the open grave.

But there are other ways of dying, and bells tolled
for executions. At the Old Bailey, when the prisoner, who
stood in the dock, scattered with rue to keep off gaol fever,
was sentenced to death, as the Clerk of the Court said
"What have you to say why judgment of death and execution should not be awarded against you", a noose of whipcord was slipped over his thumbs by the executioner, and
tightened so that he should know in which way he was
to die. Then he was imprisoned in one of the condemned
cells at Newgate. Howard in 1784 described these fifteen
cells: they were nine feet long by six feet broad, the
vaulted roof was nine feet high at the top of the vault, the
doors were four inches thick, and the stone walls lined
with planks studded with broad-headed nails; there was
a wooden bed in each cell, and each was lighted by a
window three feet by one and a half feet, barred with a
double grating. He says: "I was told by those who attended

them that criminals, who had affected an air of boldness during their trial and appeared quite unconcerned at the pronouncing sentence upon them, were struck with horror and shed tears when brought to these darksome solitary abodes."

In 1605 Robert Dowe gave a donation to the Parish of St. Sepulchre's, which with other charities was recorded on a board fixed to the wall behind the altar—"Mr. Robert Dowe gave for ringing the greatest bell in this church on the day the condemned prisoners are executed and for other services, for ever, concerning such condemned prisoners, for which services the sexton is paid £1 6s. 8d." On the Sunday before Black Monday, the condemned prisoners were taken to chapel, and sat round an open coffin to listen to a sermon. Afterwards, friends came for the last time, and gave them a white cap with black ribbons, a nosegay, a Prayer Book, and an orange, to scent the tainted air. That night, as they sat or lay in their cells, they would hear a handbell ringing in the street, and then the parish clerk of St. Sepulchre's would cry out this exhortation:

"You prisoners that are within, who for wickedness and sin after many mercies shown you are now appointed to die tomorrow in the forenoon; give ear and understand that, tomorrow morning the greatest bell of St. Sepulchre's parish shall toll for you from six till ten, in order and manner of a passing bell, which used to be tolled for those which lie at the point of death, to the end that all godly people hearing that bell, and knowing it is for you going to your deaths, may be stirred up to hearty prayer to God to bestow His grace and mercy upon you, whilst you yet live. Seeing the prayers of others will do you no good, unless you turn to God, in true sorrow for your sins, and pray with them for yourselves also, I beseech you all, and every one of you for Jesus Christ's sake, to keep this night in watching and hearty prayer to God for the salvation of your own soul, whilst there is yet time and place for mercy, as knowing that tomorrow you must appear before the judgment-seat of your Creator, there to give an account of all things done in this

79

life, and to suffer eternal torment for your sins committed against Him, unless upon your hearty and unfeigned repentance you obtain mercy, through the merits and death and passion of Jesus Christ, your only Mediator and Redeemer, who came into the world to save sinners, and now sits at the right hand of God to make intercession for you, if you penitently return to Him. So, Lord have mercy upon you, Lord have mercy upon you all."

Then the clerk would recite this poem:

All you that in the condemned hold do lie,
Prepare you for tomorrow you shall die;
Watch all, and pray, the hour is drawing near
That you before the Almighty must appear;
Examine well yourselves, in time repent,
That you may not to eternal flames be sent.
And when St. Sepulchre's bell tomorrow tolls,
The Lord above have mercy on your souls.

Next morning the prisoners were taken into the room next the gate of the prison; some would be gay, others would be saying long extempore prayers, and assisted to repentance by Silas Todd; others may have looked like Governor Wall, sentenced to death in 1802 for unjustly causing a soldier called Benjamin Armstrong to be beaten to death with 800 lashes of inch-thick rope at Goree in 1782. and who when led out to be pinioned "was death's counterfeit, tall, shrivelled and pale; and his soul shot so piercingly through the portholes of his head, that the first glance of him nearly terrified me". Then they were taken out in the cart, and at the steps of St. Sepulchre's they were given another nosegay; the last to receive it was Sixteen String Jack, who was hanged for robbing the Rev. Dr. Bell of his watch and eighteenpence at Gunnersbury Lane in 1774; and with the great bell tolling above them, the parish clerk ringing his handbell, with the beadle of Merchant Taylors Hall to see he did his duty, would say his last admonition.

"All good people pray heartily to God for these poor sinners going to their deaths, and for whom this great bell

doth toll; and you that are condemned to die, repent yourselves with lamentable tears, and ask mercy of the Lord for
the salvation of your own souls, through the mercies, death
and passion of Jesus Christ, your only Mediator and Redeemer, who came into the world to save sinners, and now
sits at the right hand of God to make intercession for you,
if you heartily return to Him. So Lord have mercy upon
you, Lord have mercy upon you all."

Then the cart went on past the confession sellers, ballad
sellers, gin sellers, and gingerbread sellers to Tyburn, where
the toughs kicked off their shoes, as they were turned off,
and their friends hung on their legs.

Besides these tolls and chimes and peals for the services
of the church and for individuals when they were married
or interred, there were as well, Feast Days, when the bells
would be rung in special ways. In Advent, when the pace
of religious life speeds up after a succession of Trinity
Sundays, the bells were rung once in the first week, and
so on till the last, when they rang four times. At Wragby
in Lincolnshire on St. Thomas's Day in the last week of
Advent, the tenor bell rang to call the poor of the parish
to the church to receive a dole of bread and meat from the
churchwardens; but this was discontinued in 1877, and the
other Advent peals became submerged by the weekly
practices.

Christmas and Christmas Eve are still great times for
ringing; at Dewsbury in Yorkshire, while their children
were eating Yule babies, sticky representations of a child
in cake, the ringers would toll the Devil's Knell to announce
his death at the Birth of Christ. But today ringing is much
the same as at any other time of the year. On Christmas
Eve ringers come to raise the bells, perhaps leaving them
set all night, so that at six o'clock next morning they will
have less work to do on empty stomachs. The belfry
seems more attractive at night, especially if lit with oil
lamps and the walls painted with pink wash, so that the
ringers' waistcoats have the soft sheen of a scarab beetle's
back. After a touch they will leave the church, coming

back in the early morning to ring before the first Communion service. On Boxing Day, it is customary in some parishes for them to collect money at each house in payment for the pleasure which they have given in the course of the year.

At Basingstoke, until the last war, a hymn would be sung on top of the tower after the service on New Years' Eve, and then the bells would ring in the New Year. Other towers ring out the Old Year with a half-muffled peal, and then take the pads off the clappers and ring in the New. St. Paul's Cathedral is still a gathering-place for the Scots on this night, and they stand in the street, waving bottles of whisky. The tension mounts, till everyone is silent, gazing up at the foggy façade as the quarter bells strike before the hour. Midnight itself strikes, and Auld Lang Syne is sung; but after the last stroke of twelve no more music comes from the bells. Since the war, the New Year has not been rung in at St. Paul's.

Lent, like New Year's Eve at St. Paul's today, was silent; from Ash Wednesday the bells would not be rung; though at Cottingham in Northamptonshire one bell was tolled every day at eleven in the morning, and for this service to the parish, the ringer was given eggs on Easter Day. Good Friday was another day of silence, except perhaps in Scotland. Dunbar in "The Flyting of Dunbar and Kennedie" has these two lines:

> Ane benefice quha wald gyve sic any beste,
> Bot gif it was to gyngill Judas bellis.

These Judas bells are still rung in Malta to execrate the memory of Judas Iscariot; the Maltese also have wooden rattles, which they twirl round to represent the rattling of his bones which never rest in the grave.

Up to the beginning of the nineteenth century and in some cases to an even later date, the day began and ended in many parishes with the ringing of a bell. In 1399, Bishop Arundel ordered that the Gabriel bell, which rang in the evening to remind people to say an Angelus, should also ring in the morning, when an Ave and a Paternoster should be said. Curfew, which was instituted by a law of William I, was repealed by Henry I. Pope John XXII, at the beginning of the fourteenth century, ordered an Ave and an Angelus to be said when the Gabriel bell was rung at eight or nine o'clock in the evening. Although curfew was repealed, and the Reformation did away with the saying of Aves, Paternosters, and Angeluses, the bells continued to be rung as a signal to start and end each day. Even before the Reformation the Morning Bell had been adapted to secular use, for in 1467 at Worcester it was ordained that labourers wishing to be hired should be at the Grass Cross when it rang at five in the morning in summer and at six in winter. Queen Elizabeth, in 1583, passed an order that when curfew rang in the evening the public-houses should close, and in Bristol, in 1500, the Mayor proclaimed that "at Christmas no one of any degree or condition may go mumming after curfew from St. Nicholas without a light, either sconce, lantern, candle or torch". But soon people found that it was more fun to sit up late at night and get up late in the morning than to get up at five and go to bed at eight, though two people with 120 years between them left money in their wills to keep up the tradition. Margery Dubbleday —she was a washerwoman—died in 1544 and gave to St. Peter's Nottingham, a bell inscribed: "Ave Maria of your charitie for to pray for the sole of Margere Dubbleday." She also left the rent of a piece of land amounting to a pound a year to pay the sexton for ringing her bell every morning, except Sundays, at four o'clock. Richard Palmer, in 1664, gave land to the church at Wokingham so that money from it could pay the sexton for ringing the bell at four o'clock in the morning and eight o'clock at night, so that the parishioners might be guided home and encouraged to early rising and thoughts of their resurrection.

In the same way sloth had its supporters. The apprentices of Cheapside are commemorated in the rhyme about

Bow Bell which used to ring at nine o'clock at night; the apprentices were supposed to say:

Clarke of the Bow Bell, with the yellow locks.
For thy late ringing thy head shall have knocks.

To which the clerk replied:

Children of Chepe hold you all still,
For you shall have Bow Bell rung at your will.

A more effective protest than this one against a survival of curfew was made by Dr. Martin and Lady Arabella Howard at the end of the seventeenth century. They lived close to the church at Hammersmith, and every morning they were woken by the bell at five o'clock. They secured an injunction against this ringing during their lives, on condition that they gave a new clock, a bell, and a cupola to the church, which they did, and so slept out their morning sleep in peace. The Morning bell died out because people did not like to be woken up so early, or because the sexton was too lazy. Curfew survived for longer, and is still rung in some places. It ceased to ring at Chiswick because the parish refused to pay the ringer, while at Kidderminster it continued to ring because a man who lost his way returning from a fair at Bridgnorth heard the bell and was guided safely home. It is still rung in London at Lincoln's Inn, and also in Oxford, where Great Tom of Christ Church rings each night finishing with 101 strokes, the original number of members of the foundation.

Other bells regulated other actions of parochial life. The Mote or Common bell, hung either in one of the churches or in the Guild Hall, was rung to bring the people together for secular gatherings. At Stamford it tolled at 10.45 a.m. on November 13th to start the bull running, and other towns rang their Mote bell to warn the corporation of the election of the mayor. The treble or the tenor would be rung to call the vestrymen together for their meetings. At Beverley a bell warned the parishioners to pay their church rents. At Totnes in Devon church bells announced

84

Council meetings, and at Goldington in Bedfordshire, when an inquest was being held, the Death Knell was not rung in case the verdict was suicide; for murder, or death by natural causes or any other decision, the Death Knell was rung after the inquest.

The lord of a manor had the curious feudal right to insist that all the bread in the parish was baked in his oven, and an Oven bell was a warning that it was hot and ready for the dough. Sir Matthew Lamb, Lord of the Manor of Melton Mowbray, endeavoured in the eighteenth century to enforce his right to do this, but he gave up the attempt in 1780. In some parishes a bell was rung at the end of the Morning Service, as an indication that there would be another later in the day. Where the baker cooked dinners in his slowly cooling oven it became known as a Pudding bell, and when he heard it he would prepare to take out the joints of mutton and beef. St. Helen's, Worcester, rang a bell called a Pie bell between midday and one o'clock on Christmas.

Before the inevitable domination of this country by middlemen, markets were started with the ringing of a bell to prevent traders forestalling, engrossing, regrating, and badgering. "Forestalling" was buying up goods before a market with a view to enhancing their price; "engrossing" was to buy wholesale for the purpose of "regrating" or selling at monopoly prices; three words with a very similar implication. "Badgering" is the same, and the "badger" was a licensed middleman who would buy goods from people and sell them at a profit in the market. The *Oxford English Dictionary* has many definitions of the badger, and his name is possibly derived from the broad white streaks on his face, a badgard, and less probably from the French *blaireau*, a diminutive of *blaier*, meaning a little corn merchant; supporting this is the remark of Littré's that "the badger makes away with much buckwheat". In England badgers were licensed and dealt in corn, fish, butter and cheese—"our butter fetches a penny a pound more than other peoples from the Badger". And in Lancashire he was a keeper of a small provision shop, a most suitable occupation for this plump and kindly animal. (Looking up Badger in the dictionary leads one to other, smaller animals, voles for instance; and here there are some fine remarks. "May the vole-plague ravage the land of those who neglect this plain featured fact." "A committee of gentlemen who had come specially to investigate the vole question", and "The economic vole inhabits a sort of oven-shaped chamber".)

Agriculture was also controlled by bells. In the mornings when seed for the year's harvest was sown, a bell would ring and those hunched figures with one arm thrown back would walk up and down the fields; later they would carry a fiddle slipping the seed out mechanically. When the corn was cut a bell would both start and end gleaning for the day, so that everyone would have a fair chance, and at Louth in Lincolnshire a bell rang when the harvest was ripe on a field called the "Gatherums", and the poor for whom it was grown were then allowed to pick it. A Harvest Home bell tolled when the last wagon, decorated with boughs of oak and ash, rolled home to the farm laden with the last sheaves of corn. After the harvest, when the wagons were no longer being used for carrying corn, on Boon Days a bell would ring to tell their owners that this was the day when their wagons were at the service of the parish to carry stone from the quarry to the road.

Another bell heard occasionally before the Industrial Revolution in England was the Tocsin. This was one special bell in the tower which was rung with the others in changes, but when rung by itself with the rhythm used by firemen today was a warning against fire, invasion, or other disasters. In Sherborne Abbey a bell exclusively used for a fire alarm was inscribed:

J W I C 1652

Lord quench this furious flame,
Arise, run, help, put out the same.

86

Ringing "backwards" was also a form of alarm, when the bells instead of ring rounds would ring up the scale, starting with the tenor and finishing with the treble.

The Imperial Institute in South Kensington has a ring of ten bells hanging two hundred feet above the ground. They were given by Mrs. Elizabeth Millar of Melbourne, Australia, to the President of the Institute, Edward VII when he was Prince of Wales, on condition that they should ring on royal occasions; the funerals of princes and their obits again. Unfortunately the tower sways a foot out of the vertical when they ring, so they can only be heard at these royal times. Another gift, though of a different kind, was the legacy of Thomas Nashe of Bath, who left £50 a year to the ringers of the Abbey bells on the condition that:

> "They ring all the bells muffled to solemn and doleful changes with rests for refreshment from eight o'clock in the morning until eight in the evening on the 14th May being the anniversary of his wedding day; and on the day of his death a grand Bob Major and merry mirthful peals un-muffled in commemoration of my happy release from Domestic tyranny and wretchedness."

There is a reference in this bequest to a mysterious divine who was also to benefit from his death:

> "The Rev. ———— of ———— may resume his amatory labours without enveloping himself in a sedan chair for fear of detection."

There are many similar cases of money being left so that ringers could celebrate events with a peal. On October 7th, the ringers of Twyford in Hampshire have a feast paid from the legacy of a man who when riding home at night heard the bells ringing and changed direction just in time to avoid going over the edge of a chalk-pit; if ever the peal is forgotten the feast will lapse.

A woman lost her way one night near Wingrave in Buckinghamshire, but she heard the bell and came home safely. As a thank-offering, she gave a piece of marshy land to provide clean rushes for the floor of the church, and every year hay is cut on St. Peter's Day and strewn on the floor.

At Harlington in Middlesex, the rent from half an acre of land called Pork Half-acre buys a leg of pork, which the ringers eat on the evening of November 5th, provided they have shot Old Guy in the morning to celebrate the deliverance of parliament from the Gunpowder Plot. No one knows who provided this feast, for in 1805 the rector tore up all the deeds belonging to the church. "Shooting Old Guy" was to ring the bells in rounds and then "fire" them. Parliament ordered that its deliverance on this night should be celebrated, and it is possible that the all-night ringing on the vigil of All Saints, stopped by Henry VIII, may have attached itself to this new feast; up till the middle of the last century Guy Fawke's Day was always celebrated with ringing as well as peals, and in the West Country it was known as "Bell Ringing Night".

Other celebrations were stopped by the Puritans; in 1644 Parliament ordered that all the maypoles should be taken down. A few survived, and at Bytham in Lincoln-shire their maypole was preserved in the church, made into one of the ladders up to the belfry with this inscription carved on it: "This ware the May Poul 1660." But the original May Day celebrations were in some instances transferred to May 29th, the day Charles II rode over London Bridge on his restoration to the throne, which was celebrated with as much joy as the execution of his father with mourning (at Newcastle-upon-Tyne, the bells rang a muffled peal on January 30th for many years). On May 29th at Whitchurch Canonicorum men went out into the woods at three in the morning and cut down boughs of oak and put one on the church tower and another on a post in the village; then they rang the bells, and afterwards decorated each house with a bough hung over the porch. One bell at least, however, the treble at Witham-on-the-Hill in Lincolnshire, is against almost everything:

> 'Twas not to prosper pride or hate
> William Augustus Johnson gave me,
> But peace and joy to celebrate
> And call to prayer to heaven to save ye:
> Then keep the terms and e'er remember,
> May 29th, ye must not ring
> Nor yet the 5th of each November
> Nor on the crowning of a king.
>
> 1831.

Only one of these ancient ringing occasions still flourishes, the annual Shrove Tuesday pancake race at Olney in Buckinghamshire. Shrove Tuesday was the day before the beginning of Lent when the whole parish would be shriven by the priest, and supposedly the day for eating the last stocks of butter and other perishable foodstuffs before the forty-day fast. The bell which rang to call the people to church became in time the signal for the day's festivities to begin, it was called the Pan Burn Bell at Daventry, the Fritter Bell in Maidstone, or the Guttit Bell in Cheshire; the Pancake Bell is the usual name. The apprentices of York held the right to enter the Minster and ring this to start the holiday, and in Northamptonshire there is an appropriate bell rhyme:

> Pancakes and fritters
> Say the bells of St. Peter's.
> Where must we fry 'em
> Say the bells of Cold Higham.
> In yonder land furrow
> Say the bells of Wellingborough.

Taylor the Water Poet gives a description of Shrove Tuesday and of the pancakes which were eaten.

"Shrove Tuesday, at whose entrance in the morning all the whole kingdom is in quiet, but by the time the clock strikes eleven, which (by the help of a knavish sexton) is commonly before nine, there is a bell rung called pancake bell, the sound whereof makes thousands of people distracted and forgetful either of manners or humanity. Then there is a thing called wheaten flour, which cooks do mingle with water, eggs, spice and other tragical magical enchantments, and then they put it by little and little into a frying pan of boiling suet, there it makes a confused dismal hissing (like the lernain snakes in the reeds of Acheron) until at last, by the skill of the cook it is transformed into the form of a flip-jack called a pancake, which ominous incantation the ignorant people do devour very greedily."

Nobody knows when or why the first pancake race was run at Olney; one date is 1445, and two origins are that a woman making pancakes heard the shriving bell and rushed off to the church with her frying-pan, and another is that the pancakes are a bribe for the verger to ring the bell earlier than he should so the holiday might start. There have been times when the race was not run, but after the 1939-45 war it was revived by the vicar. In 1949, the Junior Chamber of Commerce of Liberal, Kansas, in the United States of America, was searching for a way of bringing their town to the notice of the world, and finally decided to challenge the women of Olney as to who could win a race run over the same distance carrying a frying-pan complete with pancake. The prize was a pressure cooker, which was won by Olney for the first time in 1950, again they won in 1951, but lost in 1952. In 1953, the race was billed as the "First Great Event of Coronation Year" on the orange stickers for the windscreens of motor-cars, which bore also a picture of two ladies in wimples carrying long-handled pans towards a Norman church door.

On the day of the race Olney was *en fête,* the square in the centre of the town was decorated with Union Jacks and the Stars and Stripes, and a few members of the American Air Force were walking round with their beautiful German cameras; one had come specially to Olney because he was a native of Liberal. Boy Scouts, choir-boys, and ladies in Tudor costume were selling programmes in the street. By eleven o'clock the town was full of cars, and of charabancs called "Pancake Special". There were two warning bells struck on the tenor, and at the second the competitors came out into the square, where the race starts. According to the rules of the race, they must wear the traditional costume of a housewife, including apron and head-covering. The aprons were flowery cotton or plastic, and for this year some were specially made with red, white and blue edges, with a Union Jack sewn into the centre. The older competitors interpret head-covering as a hat, but the young women's heads were turbanned up in scarves, some wore gym shoes to get a good grip on the slippery asphalt, and all carried their frying-pans. Some of these were enamelled green and cream, others were of thick and serviceable aluminium, but the pancakes were all the same, not the wafer-thin delights, dimpled by hot butter and spotted like the pard, which can be blown off the plate they are so light, the perfect medium for sugar and lemon juice, but thick, heavy confections. Undoubtedly the women of Olney make the most ethereal pancakes at other times, but today only a heavy pancake will stay securely at the bottom of the pan.

By this time the representatives of the newspapers had arrived, the cameraman pursued by troops of admiring children, who would easily be persuaded to carry step-ladders and boxes, while a black leather motor-cyclist stood by to rush the pictures back to London. The spectators meekly lined the kerb along the course, the competitors stood in a line across the start, but the photographers milled and bunched all over the road, dominating the entire scene. After they had taken control to their satisfaction, they organised a few practise starts, so that they could take their pictures in comfort, and then they allowed the race to begin. A Beefeater with a partisan rang a bell above the women, crouched for a sprinting start, each with a thumb firmly holding the pancake in place, and off they went at a killing pace on their way to the church door.

The path from the gate into the churchyard to the porch was lined with spectators, kept in position by old bell ropes looped from gravestone to gravestone. At the church door behind the verger and the vicar stood the choir in violet cassocks and surplices with white ruffles at the neck, the girls in "Canterbury Caps" and the boys' hair nicely brilliantined in place. Soon the leaders came flashing down the path, the cameras whirred and clicked, and before you could say "Jack Robinson" the winner was hidden by a solid press of overcoats and mackintoshes finding out her name and the time (1 minute 7·2 seconds for the 415 yards) from the time-keeper, who came in on a bicycle from the starting point so that he could reach the finish before the runners. The winner received a kiss of peace from the verger, and then there was a Shriving Service, the hymns being two of those written by William Cowper when he lived at Olney, and by John Newton, the slave-trader turned parson, who was vicar in Cowper's time.

The prize was presented at the west door of the church and here everyone else gathered, including an air-hostess from an American airline who had come with a special pancake recipe. The door opened, and the altar glowed far away in the darkness of the church, lit with more candles than St. Peter's. The vicar, the verger, and a representative of the American Embassy presented the winner with a pressure cooker, while the children of the losers stood around eating the remains of their mothers' pancakes. Later that night there was a Shrovetide Dance—Old Time —when the winner received the International Trophy, an engraved skillet.

Kings and Queens of England have special bells rung for them at their deaths and special ways of ringing to mark their Coronations. When a member of the Royal Family dies, the hour bell of St. Paul's chimes for one hour; and when the monarch dies it chimes for two. The Sebastopol bell at Windsor Castle is only rung when the monarch dies, and at no other time.

The wildest ringing is for Coronations. On these infrequent days members of the Ancient Society of College Youths wait in the belfry at Westminster Abbey. Here the street decorations in 1953 were formal and magnificent, of the Field-of-the-Cloth-of Gold-type, with the symbols of the Government offices and the heraldry of the Commonwealth. Farther away, each municipality took over with varying success, thin streamers in Holborn giving place to "olde scrolles" with "We hope you will visit St. Pancras again". Behind the pavements are the houses, each decorated according to the fancy of the owner, so that London was a mixture of private enterprise and planning, private enterprise mostly winning æsthetically, though surprisingly those forts of conservatism, the large blocks of flats, often had no decoration at all. The happiest co-operation was achieved in the eighteenth- and nineteenth-century suburbs of North-east London, particularly in Chapel Market and the courts leading off it, in Godson Street, and Grant Street. Grant Street has cast-iron balconies, and below the bunting and pennants these gleamed, each piece of iron wrapped round with red, white, and blue—a single balcony may have cost as much as two pounds ten shillings to decorate—receding points of light on each side of the road. Chapel Market is a street where cabbages, plaster Sealyhams, and old magazines are sold from barrows, and it was so strung with pennants that the sky vibrated. Each house and shop had a patriotic window display, and in the centre of the road, half-way down, was a square double-sided altar, wrapped with red, white, and blue round the plinth, then banked hydrangeas and geraniums, and, back to back below a *baldacchino* of white bunting, two portraits—" 'er one side, 'im and 'er on the other". The jewels hidden in this rich setting were the courts leading off the market's southern side. Some of these were scheduled for demolition thirty days after the Coronation, and the inhabitants had dressed up their homes for this last great event they were to celebrate there; even the lamp-posts were wreathed round with gold paper. But the supreme achievement was Godson Street. Here the sky was hidden with pale mauve, green, yellow, and blue silk pennants, shimmering in the wind; a stage had been built for the children's party, paper crowns hung above the pavement —there is no road—each house displayed a portrait decked round with paper. Stamped decorations in gold paper which had been bought from Woolworth's were stained for added richness, and at one end was the best-decorated house in London. Outside, the low wall below the railings had been painted red, white, and blue, as were the spear-heads of the railings. The lower floor of the house was bright red, and on it were placed artificial flowers, pictures of the Queen, and cardboard crowns. Above this on either side of the windows hung tall panels of gold paper with more artificial flowers, and in front on poles tied to the railings were large fat crowns, set with pieces of looking-glass. The whole a wonderful mass of ornament which had achieved that perfection, rarely reached, when clutter becomes complexity and over-elaboration is richness.

This, then, was the setting on the ground for the ringers who "fire" the bells at a Coronation. Sometimes bells are fired for weddings, but, as is often the case with bells, that sloth which is too slothful to seek pleasure, frequently prevents the bells in this country being rung joyfully. The seekers after the folky eagerly revive folk-dancing or meticulous peasant embroidery and intellectuals flock to Mexico or Congo to enrich their lives; it is easy to neglect the urge for jollity and fun which lies under our own noses.

5

The Bell Foundry

WORKING metals is a grimy job. The cold intractability of iron is felt as much in the smallest garage whose doors are covered with rusty tin-plate advertisements as in the great sheds of a factory making naval guns. The lathes and drills and planes may be painted bright colours by the industrial psychologist, strains of old Vienna can boom through loud-speakers, but nothing dispels the black dust and grit lying on the floor and hanging in the air.

The bell-foundry is a long shed with whitewashed brick walls powdered with dust. In the roof are skylights of smoky glass, and the floor is earth except where it is covered with boards of steel. Little cupboards hang on one wall, in which the men keep their teacups and snacks; one is a first-aid box of bandages and burn dressings. Nearby is a gas-ring for making tea, and above, hanging from bars, are the steel hooks and clamps used in the work, hard-edged and rusty red. At one end is a kiln with a low-vaulted brick ceiling, and a steel door which rises vertically on counterweights. A brazier of coke burns here in the winter, and it is a warm and comfortable place to sit. Against the other wall is a row of wooden bunkers filled with yellow London clay and dry flakes of grey mud; gardeners' sieves stand on the floor, and close to the bunkers is a wide bench where the loam is made for the moulds. The furnace is a cube of whitewashed brick at the opposite end of the foundry to the kiln, and beside it is a pit where the largest bells are cast.

The mould for a bell is in two parts, the core which shapes the inside, and the cope, a shell forming the outside; when the cope is placed over the core, it leaves a space the exact shape of the bell. Thinking of a space which is soon to become a solid object is not easy, but if a flower-pot with a diameter of four inches was put mouth downwards on the ground and covered by another pot with a diameter of five inches, they would be exactly like a bell mould. The small one inside is the core, and the large one outside the cope. If the hole in the little pot was filled up and molten metal poured into this horticultural mould, it would run between the two, harden and become a crude bell. The core and the cope are modelled in loam; London clay, manure, and hair mixed with water, it can be used again and again, if each time a little new clay is added to give it strength. This compost is worked with a tool like a long spade, but only two or three inches wide; smacked down on the loam, a rich plum-pudding, it slops and squishes on the table, wet and shiny.

When a bell-founder designs a ring or adds a new bell to an old one, he controls the note of each so that they will be in tune by varying the thickness of the metal and the diameter at the lip, and to make the space between the two parts of the mould into the shape he desires, the cope and the core are modelled with a tool called a gauge. This is a strip of metal cut to represent a section taken from the crown to the lip of the bell, bolted to a long metal

Copes in the Foundry.

97

rod pointed at either end. The outer profile moulds the cope and the inner profile the core. The core is built on a round iron plate with a large hole cut out of the centre, lying on a small trolley called a carriage so that it can be easily moved from place to place. The gauge works like a compass: one arm is the iron bar which passes vertically through the hole in the plate and rests on a socket at the centre of the carriage. The other arm is the gauge itself, swinging round the bar to trace in air the inside profile of the bell. The top of the compasss is held by a long arm which swings out from a pillar standing close to the wall.

The man making the core carries a bucket of loam to the carriage. He takes a handful and throws it down on to the plate between the edge of the hole and the knife-like blade of the gauge, then scrapes some off with his fingertips and throws it down again, to form an even, consistent layer with no air pockets. The wet slapping of loam is a sound continually heard when the moulds are being made. Then he takes small curved bricks and, from the edge of the hole in the plate to within an inch of the gauge, lays the first course of a wall, which will follow the gauge up its whole height, always keeping an inch from it, till a tiny brick tower has been built sloping inwards, the bricks bound together with loam for mortar, and forming a strong basis for the final covering.

At night the core will be wheeled into the kiln to dry; not subjected to the intense heat of the kilns used for firing pottery, but dried by a fire of coke which burns in a pit sunk into the floor. Sometimes, when travelling in a train which has stopped on an embankment above a manufacturing town, smoke suddenly spurts up through the roof of a building. "Ah," you think, "a fine view of a fire"; but no one makes a fuss, there are no fire-engines, no heroic jets of water. It's only Old Bodger's number two pot disgorging another thousand plastic toasting forks. At the foundry this rich effulgence of smoke streams out when the brazier is emptied into the pit in the kiln, and stoked to keep the fire burning through the night.

Next morning when the core is wheeled out of the kiln, any dust is blown away with a pair of bellows, and it is then watered with a watering-can. More loam is thrown on the bricks, scraped off and thrown down again, not built right up to the curve traced by the gauge, but puddled all over with thumb-prints, black dimples which form a key for the last layer. For this, the gauge is constantly in use; it is moved slowly round, scraping away the surplus, like the blade of a knife scraping butter. The air cut by the gauge becomes a solid of clay, manure, hair, and bricks, rising from the steel plate, higher and higher, round and round; a perfectly smooth, even curve, almost horizontal at the top and unbroken except where the bar runs down through the centre to the carriage. Then the gauge is removed, and the core is pushed into the kiln to dry for the last time.

The cope is made inside an iron case roughly the shape of a bell and perforated in a regular pattern of small holes which the clay squeezes through like toothpaste. At the narrow end of the case is a collar about six inches high, flattened at its rim so that it can be stood upside down; there is another rim at the wide opening. This case is stood on a carriage, wide mouth upwards, and the gauge used for the core is fitted inside, only this time it is the other way up. The point of the bar which before was held by the arm coming out from the pillar now rests on the socket in the middle of the carriage, and the other point is held at the centre of a strip of steel passing across the mouth of the case and bolted to the flange, so that the gauge can turn round defining the outer curve of the bell. If there is too big a gap between the gauge and the case, it is filled in with bricks to within an inch of the gauge. If the loam is too thick, the molten metal poured into the mould will compress the clay, and it will not harden with sufficient density, giving the bell a poor tone. If the clay is too thin, the metal can crack it, and form scabs on the outside of the bell where it has forced itself into the fissures in the clay.

The first layer of loam is laid down so that it just clears the gauge, and left as before with thumb prints all over the rich shiny black surface. Making a cope is a more arduous affair than making a core. The workman has to stand on the carriage, and lean right inside the case to start work at the bottom. If it is a very large bell, he will be standing on his head clinging to the bar carrying the gauge with one hand, while he slaps and moulds the loam with the other. If he is making an enormous bell, he can stand inside the cope and work there, but always the cope has to be *right;* roughness on the inside of a bell can be cut away when it is tuned, but the outside must be crisp and clear, and this can only be achieved by perfection. The second layer of loam will again just clear the gauge, and is left not with the deep depressions of innumerable thumbs but finely combed with the tips of the fingers into a series of ridges rising up from the bottom; for that is the easiest way to bring them, and then higher up where it is possible to work by just leaning over the rim of the case, swept round in circles right to the top. Like the core, the copes are dried in the kiln at various stages of their manufacture, and puffed with a bellows to blow away the dust and watered with the can before more loam is added. The last layer is smoothed evenly away by the gauge which has on this side two ridges near the shoulder of the bell, and two more near the lip which dig little troughs to form the wires. After the last layer has been applied, the gauge is removed and washed so that it shall be clean and sharp for the last time it is used. For now the loam is exactly shaped by it, and to make the surface absolutely smooth like a new pat of butter, washes of loamy water are brushed on, filling in any little pits and smoothing down any traces of projecting hair. When these have dried a bag filled with graphite, like a black powder-puff, is tapped all over the surface of the mould; the graphite rubbed into the loam leaves the surface smoother even than it was before. Bell metal is an alloy of copper and tin, but when it is poured into the moulds the tin tries to seep into the clay, but the graphite helps to prevent this.

The inside of the cope is now a smooth, dully gleaming surface. Soft still, because it has not been dried out in the kiln since the last layer of loam and the thin washes were added to it. The surface is unmarked except where the wires leave two pairs of concentric rings. Now is the time for the inscription and any bas-relief decoration to be stamped into the still yielding mould. The gauge is taken out and the clamps which hold the case to the carriage are knocked off. The overhead crane is brought over, and from its hook two chains dangle down; these catch two projections which stick out like the stalk and knob of a front collar-stud, slightly below half-way down on each side of the cope. The cope is now hoisted up, and hangs horizontally from the chains, in an easy working position for the spacing and stamping of the inscription.

So that the lettering will be parallel with the wires, a special compass is used, and so adjusted that it will describe accurately circular lines on the surface of the mould. The surface is given a light dusting with the graphite bag, and when the metal letter punches are gently pressed into the graphite, they leave a clear impression and the spacing can be worked out accurately. Then the punches are lightly tapped with a hammer, leaving their mark on the resisting loam. In the early days of bell-founding the founder sometimes forgot to put all the inscription in reverse so that when he opened the mould after casting, before an admiring throng, he would find that the inspiring words "Com when I call to serve God" looked like this: "ƆOM when I ɔall to serve Ɔob." After the inscription, any decoration is stamped on in the same way, the foundry mark and the date are added, and the work of making the moulds is nearly finished.

Before the cope can be lowered over the core, there are two more jobs to be done. The bar of the gauge has left a hole in the top of the core which has to be filled in; to do this a circular piece of wood is twisted round and round into the hole until it rests on the bricks in the centre. The wood is now covered with loam.

Small bells when they are cast can be lifted by catching them with hooks under the lip, but this cannot be done with a really large bell, so a nut is placed on the centre of wood resting on the bricks, and then covered up with the loam till the top of the core is smooth. When the bell is cast a bolt can be put through the hole for the clapper staple and screwed into this nut, so that the hook from the crane can then catch the curved top of the bolt and lift the bell.

There is also a hole at the narrow end of the cope, which is filled in with a large plug of baked loam that has in it four holes, one large one in the centre for the clapper staple, with a small hole on one side of this and two small holes on the other. The two small ones allow the metal to run in—a running head—and the single small one allows the gas given off to escape and the metal to run out when the mould is full—a rising head. This plug is fixed into the top of the cope with loam, and then smoothed off with washes and graphite in the same way as the rest of the cope.

Dust is blown out of the cope with a pair of bellows, and the inside painted with thin oil, to stop any moisture being driven out of the loam by the heat of the metal. The cope and the core can now be joined together, the carriage with the core is chocked with wooden blocks so that it cannot move, and the cope is swung over on the crane and lowered gently down. The difficulty is to get the cope to settle evenly on the core, and to do this it is lowered till it just touches the lip of the core. It is then twisted from side to side so that the lip of the cope bites into the lip of the core, making a deposit of dust. If this is thicker on one side than the other, the men know that the cope is tilted in that direction, and one chain of the hoist is shortened. When the cope rests evenly on the core, it is lowered right down and twisted from side to side till it has bitten its way on to the core, making a firm seal between the two, and the cope and the core are clamped carefully together.

The last act which affects the shape of the bell is putting a piece of baked loam into the hole in the centre of the plug which fills in the top of the cope; this touches the core, and when the metal is run into the mould it will flow round it, leaving a hole right through the top of the bell for the clapper staple.

Now a casting head has to be made in sand. The three small holes are filled with cotton-waste, and a box of steel plates without top or bottom is placed on the flange at the top of the cope and clamped down. Then two blocks of wood are put inside this, so that one covers up the rising head and the other the running head. Oily sand is rammed down tight all round the blocks until it is level with the top of the steel box; the blocks are taken out and leave two square holes leading down to the running and rising head. The cotton-waste is taken out of these with a pair of elegant obstetrical forceps, and the mould is ready. It stands with others in a dumpy row waiting for casting.

At seven o'clock in the morning of the day that the bells are to be cast, the furnace is lit and the metal prepared. Seventeenth-century engravings show brick furnaces exactly similar to the one used in the bell-foundry today. Inside the brick cube is a shallow depression made of fire-clay, with a gutter running out at the end, and above this in the furnace roof is the flue of the chimney. The gutter is closed up by a small sliding door sealed with clay, which can be lifted to allow the molten metal to run out. In the side of the furnace is another sliding door, raised on counterweights so that the furnaceman may throw in the jagged lumps of metal. At the other side is the fire laid on fire bars with a deep pit below for the ashes. The heat and flames from the fire are drawn by the draught of the flue over the metal.

As the metal melts, the moulds receive the last rites of the foundry, the running and rising heads are sprayed with paraffin from an atomiser to make the sand cling together, and then warmed with an enormous blow-lamp, so that the metal will not strike a dead-cold surface as it runs. The head of a large bell being cast in the pit beside the furnace has had a coke brazier placed over it all night so that the sand is dry and hard. The carriages are firmly wedged so that they will not move. The ladle which carries the metal to the bells on the foundry floor is brought along on the crane, and lowered into the pit with the bell which is to be cast there and warmed with its own brazier of coke. The channels leading from the little door in the end of the furnace, to the rising head of the mould in the pit, and to the ladle are heated by playing the blow-lamp on them. The furnaceman is making the metal even hotter by throwing more coal on to the furnace fire, and the draught is so great that a large steel door leading to another part of the foundry is sucked slowly open. Water is played from a hose on to the ashes under the fire, and the steam rising through it as it burns liberates oxygen to make the metal even hotter.

At last the moment comes for seeing if the metal is of the right alloy, and the door of the furnace is opened, showing a pool of white-hot bell metal. The furnaceman stirs it with a long steel rod; then takes a ladle and dips out a sample of the metal and pours it into a shallow de-pression formed in casting sand in a battered old bucket. It spits and smokes, turning from white to red to black to green, and when it is cooled it is broken in half; if the grain of the metal is fine, then the bells can be cast; if it is coarse, more tin must be added, and beautiful ingots of glittering tin, stamped with the paschal lamb of the Cornish Tin Smelting Company, are thrown into the furnace.

Men come in from other parts of the foundry to help pour the metal into the moulds. The climax of days of work approaches, and they gather round the pit at the end of the furnace for the casting of the first bell. Almost always there are spectators for the casting of bells, a clergyman may come to see the ring for his church being made, or parties from schools; or people who have perhaps passed a steel works at night and seen the glowing rivers of slag being run from furnaces and the vast soup-tureens on railway trucks, demurely labelled "Hot Metal", shunting up and down railway lines, come to see this less-burning metal run slipperily into the moulds. The little door at the end of the furnace is opened, and out comes the metal, glowing white treacle, in every way undramatic except for the aura of heat and light surrounding it. Dross floats on its surface, and it builds up in a white-hot pool against a small metal spade which is kept across the channel like a sluice-gate. When this is withdrawn it rolls on down into the mould, crackling like frying bacon, but smelling like damp flannel singeing. The dross floating on its surface is kept back from the running head with a large steel rod which one of the men continually pushes slightly against the current of the metal, in the same way that one can play with the thick bubbles on a stream after a cottage washing-day. Sparks fly out of the rising head, and a spade is placed over this to keep them down; but after a few moments the metal comes up, too, with a rushing crackling, and the sluice-gate is again let down into the channel, stopping the flow. Another sluice-gate is immediately opened, and the white, treacly stream drops into the ladle; but even when liquid, metal is still heavy, so there are no drops to splash and spurt. Molten metal only becomes really vicious when it gets near water. Then the steam caused by the heat makes it explode.

The ladle full of metal is lifted out of the pit by the crane, and carried down the foundry to the first mould. On either side of it are small and rather rickety stools, and men stand on them, one turning the wheel which slowly tips up the ladle, while another keeps the dross from falling over the lip into the running-head with a steel rod. Smoke and a flicker of flame rise from the mouth of the mould, and the glare from the white metal lights up the faces attentive to the success of their work, and still after repeated experience conscious of the dangers which are encountered. They seem careless of all risk, but if the molten metal were to splash them it would burn through their clothes and sear into their flesh. The dark corners of the foundry are thrown into a deeper, richer gloom by the intensity of this light, and as the metal fills the mould, smoke pours from the rising head, followed by a shower of sparks, which are suppressed with the flat of a spade, and then the metal comes, bubbling and burning. Steam puffs out of the holes in the case, and when the mould is full the ladle is tipped back, leaving a cooling white drop on its lip. One of the men then takes a piece of newspaper and lights it from the flame burning at the rising head and throws it under the carriage, and the gases which have been forced out through the brickwork of the core explode like a gas-fire being lit, sending blue-green flames flickering out round the bottom of the mould. When all the bells are cast, any metal left in the ladle is tipped into a trough lined with sand, and cast into ingots to be used again. Then the ladle is tipped right up on to the floor, and the red-hot dross falls in a smoking pile.

The moulds standing in a row, smoking slightly and so hot that they cannot be touched, are transmuted: they are like nuts; nobody is interested in the shell, the kernel is all; they can only be judged when they are cracked open and one can see if the bell is sound, or flawed by some imperfection in the cope or core. But this cannot be done immediately, even when the metal has cooled sufficiently to become hard; if the cope were lifted off then, the bell would crack when the cold air struck it, in the same way that a hot glass disintegrates if it is put into cold water. When the bell is cold enough the casting head is taken off, and the masses of bell metal which filled the running- and rising-heads are given a tap with a hammer, cracking them off at the narrow point where the metal was forced through the small holes in the plug which filled the top of the cope. The sand which formed the casting-head scatters over the floor and flies up in a thick cloud of dust, for now there is not the slightest trace of moisture to bind it together. The cope is lifted off, but there is no shining bell, only a mass of black loam, dusty and dirty. This is the dirtiest part of the whole process. Dust rises in clouds as one man scrapes the bell clean with a wire brush and another cleans out the cope. Bone-dry loam is chipped off the bell in thick black scabs, filling the air with dust as it falls in a scurfy pile on the floor. At last the outside of the bell is clear, stained a beautiful black with the plumbago used on the inside of the cope, the wires at the shoulder and bottom crisp, and the inscription neatly raised, naming it with its date and makers for the rest of its life.

The three little stubs of metal left when the heads were cracked are chipped down level, and the core, which was put in to make the hole for the clapper, is withdrawn. Now the bell can be lifted up for the first time. Small bells can be lifted by putting hooks under the lip and swinging them up this way. But larger ones have a bolt put through the hole for the clapper and bolted on to the nut let into the core, and the hook of the crane attached to it. At last the bell swings in the air for the first time, but it is still dirty, for most of the core sticks to the inside. Hanging at the end of a chain, it moves down the foundry to a place where the floor is earth and not steel plates; it is lowered on to blocks of wood, detached from the tackle and pushed gently over sideways to give out its first protesting note as it strikes the floor.

Before the inside can be cleaned, the lip is lightly filed, for it is sharp and will cut anyone's hand who instinctively holds it while leaning inside, picking out the bricks and loam of the core. All the bricks are cleaned off to be used again, and the loam and dust swept up, broken with a

107

spade, new clay, dung and horsehair added to it, mixed with water, kneaded and hit with trowels, till it goes into a bucket an earthy pudding to make another bell. The bells, glowing richly black, lie on their sides in the machine shop, waiting to be drilled so that they will fit their headstocks

Nowadays bells have cast-iron headstocks except where wood has been specially ordered. The bell is held by four bolts passing through the crown and through corresponding holes in the centre of the headstock. At each end of this there are more holes, one set for the stay and another for the wheel which is fitted when the bell is in its place in the frame. Gudgeons stick out at either end, and through the very centre of its arch there is one more hole for the clapper staple. The bells, when they have had the four holes bored through their crown, are taken into another room to be tuned.

Before the scientific study of bell tuning in the nineteenth century, bells were tuned by knocking pieces off the sound bow with a chisel till the note was right, but this was a haphazard method. In the last century a Mr. Huddleston of Shaftesbury had a passion for tuning bells, spending days in various church towers chipping away, and Bilbie of Cullompton killed himself because he could not tune the last ring of bells he cast. Today tuning is more easily done. The bell is held mouth upwards in the giant chuck of a lathe working vertically instead of horizontally. It turns slowly round and round, and the cutting edge is brought closer to the inside curve till it touches and scores out strips of metal like threads of golden hair. The man superintending the tuning stands with a battery of tuning-forks laid out in a wooden box beside him.

He taps one, and leans over to listen, telling the operator of the lathe to take a little off there or here. If he is tuning a new ring of bells, they lie in a semicircle round him on the floor, and occasionally, he will walk round and hit them with a wooden mallet, to see that they concord, and

108

the foundry is filled with their ponderous booming and bonging. When the ring is tuned, they are taken, their lips carefully wrapped so that they will not be chipped, by lorry or train, to the church where the bell-hangers have been preparing the frame.

Steel is now in the ascendant above wood for making bell frames. It has, however, one great disadvantage—it must be painted and scraped regularly, which in the confined space of a church tower is not a very easy job to do thoroughly. Wood has the disadvantage that it expands and contracts with the change from dry to wet weather, twisting the bearings slightly; though this can be avoided by fitting self-aligning ball-bearings. Before they are sent to the tower, steel and wooden frames are assembled at the foundry, and then taken to pieces again. If the bells are to go in a new church with a brand-new tower, the frame for the bells will be built in as the tower climbs upwards.

Putting a new frame in an old tower is cramped and difficult work. When the old frame has been taken down, the bell-hangers in all probability, will have to start knocking holes in the walls of the tower to take the main girders of the frame. The bell-hangers of this country know more about the composition of church towers than almost anyone else. If a tower is small, they have to hammer at their chisels in the most cramped corners; sometimes they are lucky, and once they are through the hard outer surface may come upon loose rubble, which is easily moved; but in Wales and Cornwall they have to chip their way through granite, and a well-built flint tower can be almost as stubborn. Once the holes are prepared in the wall, the long supporting girders have to be hauled up and pushed far into one hole, and then back across the tower into the other, carefully levelled and cemented into position. After this the work gets easier, for all the other parts have been tried in the foundry, and fit exactly.

Some bell-hangers fit the headstocks and bearings to

the frame, run a rope through the hole for the clapper and down into the corresponding hole in the crown of the bell, and then pull it up till the bolts can be put through and tightened. Others fit the headstock to the bell and bring the two together up to the frame (then all that has to be done is to bolt the bearings on to the frame). One of the problems for a bell-founder is to make the bells swing round in the same amount of time, this is controlled by the distance from the gudgeons to the lip of the bell, if this is very short whatever the weight of the bell it will take a long time to swing round. In a ring of bells the length from gudgeon to lip is increased in the smaller, lighter bells by putting a wooden pad between the headstock and the crown to make them turn faster.

When the headstock and bell are in position, the wheel is attached to the headstock. The wheel for a bell is made in two parts, the upper part has two spokes which are parallel to each other, and when placed on either side of the headstock grip it firmly and are bolted to it; then the lower part of the wheel is bolted to the top. Now the bell can be turned round; a well-hung tenor weighing say 25 hundredweights, fitted with ball-bearings can easily be moved with one finger gently laid on a spoke of the wheel. When the wheel has been fitted the stay is attached to the other end of the headstock, the ground pulley bolted to the bottom of the frame, and then comes the clapper.

The clappers of medieval bells were held to the staple fixed into the crown of the bell by a bauderick. This was a piece of leather which passed round the staple and the stirrup-like top of the clapper; between the stirrup and the staple a piece of wood prevented the clapper dropping when the bell was inverted, and there was also a busk-board or sword, a piece of metal which was tied to the clapper and fixed to the piece of wood by a pin, keeping the clapper and bauderick rigid. The great disadvantage of this system was that the leather was continually wearing out, and so there are always many references to baudericks in churchwardens' accounts. The modern clapper swings from the staple on a steel pin, and has a grease-cap so that it will be always oily and smooth. The bell-hanger has to make sure that the clapper strikes the bell exactly on the diameter at right angles to the headstock; for if it is slightly off this line, the clapper will not hit with sufficient force to bring out the true note of the bell. At last the work of the bell-hanger is finished, and all he has to do is to drop the ropes down the holes drilled through the floors and ceilings in the tower till they reach the ringing chamber. The bells are ready, hanging in their green and red steel cage high above the bone orchard, waiting for their dedication and the first men to raise, ring, and fall them.

Vestry books and churchwardens' accounts show the forms of contract which were drawn up with the parish and the bellfounder when new bells were to be made or an old one recast, and in some cases give details of the preparations made by the village for recasting. Sometimes the record is cryptic and uninformative, and may only be one line of crabbed writing referring to the new bells, sandwiched between such trivia as "Item for ij ropes for the small feriall bellis xjd" in the fifteenth century, and rather more romantic ones in the eighteenth and nineteenth detailing the gradual extermination of birds and beasts and the administration of charity: "128 doz sparrows £2 2 0"; "Mr. Trapnill's maid a hedghog 4d"; "Joseph Cavill's daughter hedgehog 4d"—a Joseph Cavill rings the bells in the parish today; "Gave a poor woman and cheldren in distress with a pass 2/6d"; "Gave Wm and Jane Laver 68 Rodgmont by a pass 2/6d". Entries like these are interspersed with details of the maintenance of the bells, new ropes, wheels, baudericks, and oil. Sometimes the history of a bell is found in detail, as in these entries from the Vestry Book of St. Peter-upon-Cornhill. Robert Mott started the Whitechapel foundry.

1587 Sunday April 30th. Agreed that Robert Mott, bell founder should have the great bell, it being broken, to exchange for a perfect good bell and of good sound, to agree with the rest: and Mott to hang it up and take it down again at his own charge if it be not found perfect and good as to the end and term of a year and a day after it is first hanged up and so it be found perfect and good without any default as in the aforesaid Timothen. Mott to have for every hundred weight thereof Vs as for the exchange and then he is to have for the charge of hanging of it up also.

1587 Sunday June 25th. Ordered that Mott should take away the great bell that he did hang up for that it was disliked of all the parish generally. Also they decreed with him if he had a good and perfect treble, they would have one of him reasonable.

July 4th. Robert Mott the bellfounder to have his bill paid for casting the Great Bell, and for overplus of metal and for taking the bell down and hanging it up again also he stand bound for a year and a daye, as by the Churchwardens to be bounde in a bond as for the good and perfect proof of the bell well to hold.

A document dated 1283 gives an account of how money was raised for a new bell at Bridgwater in Somerset; it was collected from the parishioners and visitors to the town, and from the sale of a strange collection of hardware, leaden vessels with two trivets, one bason with laver, pots, and brass, and twelve-pence for a ring. Unfortunately, the old stories of people throwing bags of gold or silver into the furnace when the metal for the bell was being melted are largely untrue, as it is the tin which gives the tone to the bell. There was a very peculiar bell of this kind at the "World's Columbian Exposition" held in Chicago in 1894. This was the greatest of all exhibitions: vast, florid, it had all the nonsense one could possibly want, Lap villages, Viennese markets, Japanese temples and giant porcelain vases; also a collection of windmills as big as the whole South Bank at the Festival of Britain. The Columbian

Liberty Bell is best described by quoting in full the caption to its fine pale picture in *Picturesque World's Fair*:

"Not least among the ideas natural to the Columbian year, and which finally embodied themselves, was that of casting a new Liberty Bell, the very metal of which should have associations connected with the thought of liberty and a universal brotherhood. The plan of such a bell was conceived by Mr. William McDowell of New Jersey, and it was he who carried it into execution. Correspondence was entered into on an extensive scale, contributions for the bell came from hundreds and thousands of sources, and it was cast in time to be one of the features of the Exposition, occupying a prominent place on the Plaza just west of the Administration Building, and being rung on different notable occasions. Unique gifts contributed to make the composition of the New Liberty Bell remarkable. The keys of Jefferson Davis' house, pike heads used by John Brown at Harper's Ferry, John C. Calhoun's silver spoon, and Lucretia Mott's silver fruit knife, Simon Bolivar's watch chain, hinges from the door of Abraham Lincoln's house at Springfield, George Washington's surveying chain, Thomas Jefferson's copper kettle, Mrs. Parnell's ear-rings, and Whittier's pen are all among the articles melted to make the bell. Surely if there be anything in association it should always ring strong and true for liberty. It was first sounded on the occasion of the opening of the World's Congress of Religions, than which there could have been no better occasion for declaring the grandest liberty of all—liberty of thought. The bell is seven feet in height and weighs thirteen thousand pounds."

Bell-founding is one of the few crafts which were only slightly altered by the Industrial Revolution. When it became possible to make large iron castings, a steel case for the cope was introduced, until then a different technique was used for making this part of the mould. A core, however, was made in the same way as it is today, using a gauge, and when this was dry, it was coated with grease, and a complete copy of the bell built up on it in clay, again with a gauge; the inscription, modelled in wax, was let into it, and this clay bell was greased and covered with more

113

clay to form a cope. The core with its clay bell and clay cope were baked dry by lighting a fire inside the core. The cope was then gently lifted off, the clay bell broken up, and the cope put back on the core. The mould was then placed in a pit, and earth stamped down and round it so that the clay cope would not crack when the metal was run in. This method of making the mould with a waste bell is still occasionally used by the Taylor Bell Foundry; it has the great advantage that the inscription can be very carefully composed, and as wax gives a very crisp casting any decoration on the bell will be sharper than if it had been pressed into the soft clay inside the cope.

The "Bell Founders' Window" in York Minster shows the medieval method of making fairly small bells. The core was built up round a wooden rod lying horizontally between two supports, so that it could be turned round and the clay smoothed to a perfect shape. *Cire perdue* was also used; a core was built and the bell modelled on it in wax, covered with a clay cope and baked, the wax would run out through vent holes leaving room for the metal. With *cire perdue* it was possible to cast a ring of bells reasonably in tune with each other. The founder would start by making the heaviest bell and reduce the amount of wax and the diameter of the core proportionately till if he were casting a ring of eight, the treble would be made on a core half the diameter of the tenor, and half as much wax would be used to model the bell on this core.

In 1611 the second and tenor bells of Colyton Church were recast by Wiseman of Montacute, and Robert Farrant and John Sampson the churchwardens kept elaborate accounts of all the money that was spent. First Mr. Blackford was paid 1s. 6d. for going to Montacute to fetch the founder so that the recasting could be discussed at a parish meeting. Then a house had to be built for him to work in, built of laths covered with scrunch, clunch, or munch, thatched with straw; and stone was fetched to make the furnace. Bread and beer had to be given to the carpenters

114

who took the bells down from the tower, and Phillip Palfrey was paid for making the crown staples and the clappers and the iron keys for fixing the canons to the headstocks, and the gudgeons and bearings. The drawing of Marston Moretaine shows how the canons were attached to the headstocks with iron straps passing through them and tightened with iron wedges. *Tintinnalogia* gives some tips on hanging bells so that they are vertical when tightened up; if too high on one side, pads of leather should be put between the canons and the headstock. There are also some tips for polishing the gudgeons, by tying them between two boards of hardwood coated with sand which can be twisted to and fro, polishing and evenly turning the steel. The gudgeons rested on gun-metal bearings which were dovetailed into the frame, and were held in place with a wooden slab keyed down to the frame. Today if the canons are taken off a bell when it is rehung, a pad of wood is cut on one side to take their stumps and smooth on the other to rest tightly against the headstock. But taking off the canons is frowned on by the Central Council.

When the bells at Colyton were cast, Thomas Kirby went to Drayton to fetch a beam to weigh them, and John Wey made a place where this could be done. Walter Mareys kindly lent his wagon to carry the bells to the church, and when it was on its way, wreathed with flowers carrying these in state, there was a crunching of rotten timber, and the churchwardens had to include this item:

"Besides of the breaking of Walter Mareys wayne headd called the Draught, whereon the bell was drawen, wee must pay 2s 4d."

These occasions were always great times for free food and drink, especially if the bells were sent to the founder to be cast; then a happy party would go wandering round the county for days, with innumerable stops for bread and cheese and beer paid for out of the parish rates.

115

Nowadays there are only three church bell founders in England, Gillett and Johnston of Croydon, Mears and Stainbank of Whitechapel, and the Taylor Bell Foundry at Loughborough. Gillett and Johnston's firm was founded in 1844 as a clock manufactory; they started bell founding to make chimes in clocks themselves, and from this they turned to the manufacture of church bells and carillons. The history of the other two firms is more complicated for the plant and land changed hands several times. The Whitechapel foundry was started by Robert Mott in 1570, and the only move has been from the north to the south of Whitechapel Road sometime in the eighteenth century. At the present time the firm occupies two Georgian houses; pictures of bells hang on the walls with eighteenth century lists of rings cast in the foundry, and the template of Big Ben, forms an arch over the door from the street. The foundry is behind these two houses, and approached through a paved yard past bells waiting to be rehung or recast; some small bells have been turned upside down and used as flower pots. The Taylor Foundry has in the course of its history changed hands and even locality several times. It has been controlled by an unbroken succession of Taylors since about 1786, and has been at Loughborough since 1840. The architecture of the foundry offers a contrast to Whitechapel, for whereas Whitechapel is eighteenth the Taylor Foundry is nineteenth century, built of red Midland bricks instead of brown London stocks. It has its own ring of bells hung in a little tower. This is well enclosed so that the change ringers who are continually using it shall not disturb the people living in the surrounding houses.

The bell founder does not confine himself solely to the manufacture of bells. In his factory the frame, whether it be wood or steel, is prepared before it is sent to the church. The clappers are forged by the blacksmith, and gudgeons are turned and fitted to their bearings.

Wheels are made, the soling fitted to the spokes, and then the shrouding fitted neatly round.

Besides church bells, handbells are also cast. When they leave the foundry they are polished and tuned on a lathe—at Whitechapel the lathe used for this was installed in 1734—and then the leather handles and the clappers are attached to the highly polished bells. These handbells can either be used for playing tunes, when a great number will be needed, or for change ringing, when each ringer has two bells to control. As well as handbells, bells for clocks, ships; for warning or for pleasure, all come from the foundry; there is only one thing that is not made there, and that is the rope.

The rope-walk is a long narrow shed where ropes are twisted between a machine called a jack fixed at one end and a trolley running on rails. As the strands get tightened hard, the turning jack is stopped, and each strand is opened by inserting a piece of wood between the threads so that the worsted for the sally can be slipped between them. Red, white, and blue are the most popular colours; then red, white, and green; cathedrals have sallies of cardinal-coloured wool—a dark crimson; some churches have all white or all blue. Each strand takes one colour, and when the clumps of wool are all in place the jack is started again for the final hardening process, the strands spin round, and finally there are three thin ropes with monochrome sallies. The rope is rubbed down with chain-mail to take off any rough pieces, and the part above the sally rubbed with a rag soaked in size, to make the final finish hard and smooth. Lastly, the three strands are spun together to make one rope. The wool of the sally is teased out so t`at no ends are tucked in, and then it is clipped with shears like a poly-chromatic sheep to its final thickness, and the ends tapered off to meet the rope.

6

Towers and Spires

THE visitors to a church will carry the plywood ping-pong bats round the interior, identifying the good piece of carving from the bad, and sorting out the families inhabiting the tombs; but they seldom walk round the outside and admire the tracery of the belfry windows or criticise the proportion of the tower. Church towers and spires must have dominted the landscape for centuries, but even the villages have grown larger and the towns and cities have buried most of them completely; and now they can only impress us by their height when they stand on hills, as at Glastonbury, or are isolated in scattered villages, like Walpole St. Peter in Norfolk; or are like Salisbury, so tall that they dominate the iron and steel buildings around them.

Gothic architecture concentrated the eye on the altar, and this, with the exception of some Renaissance churches, has been the ideal of a church interior ever since. Conse-

quently the tower is often forgotten by the parson as well as by the visitors. If the west door is the usual entrance to the church, the base of the tower becomes the porch, fusing the temporal and the spiritual. The altar is seen at the end of the vista, and around the walls is a *mille-feuille* of notices, of elections and the meetings of the licensing justices, cards with the week's services written inside the black and red squares, and petitions for respect to the house of God. But if some other door is used as the general way into the church, this room may become a vestry or a store. If a vestry, to separate it from the nave, the tall tower arch is hung with a thick baize curtain, mulberry-coloured and bearing a design of dark pressed fleurs-de-lys; or filled in with a screen of stone or wood; and there will be cupboards full of cassocks and surplices, and a mirror hanging on one wall. If it is a store, you will see spare pews, dusty rush chairs, old bell-ropes hanging on coat hooks, and those dark green tin vases which, when fitted together on an elaborate armature of wire, stand before the pulpit at Christmas, Easter, and Harvest Festival, carrying holly, primroses, and stiff ears of corn.

The really accomplished church visitor, who must see everything, will search for the key to the door of the spiral staircase leading up the tower. Much exertion and loss of temper will be saved if he obtains it from the incumbent, instead of looking under cushions and mats, and into the drawers in the vestry filled with cardboard numbers, which can be combined into Hymn 446 in the Englich Hymnal, "O for a thousand tongues to sing, My dear Redeemer's praise."

Try to start with an early tower or two; nineteenth-century ones should only be climbed by the advanced student of churches, the treads of the stair will be insufficiently worn and there will be electric-light fittings; a gradual progression through the chronologically arranged periods of English ecclesiastical architecture is best.

If you have never been up a church tower before, stand

still when you open the door; you should hear the tick of the clock and smell a special smell of paraffin and dry wood. Up the stairs round a few turns of the spiral, a doorway opens into the ringing chamber. Restorations of the last century altered the appearance of ringing chambers in the same way that they altered the plain and decaying body of the church with embellishments of encaustic tiles and wrought-iron work. The restorers of this century continue the necessary repairs to the rooms in the tower; but given the money, they like to spend it on disclosing the original fabric and in destroying the decorations of the last century, so that soon there will not be one example of nineteeth-century adornment left. The money from innumerable whist drives and garden fêtes, besides being for the purchase of tortoise-stoves and electric apparatus for blowing the organ, has also been spent on rehanging, recasting, and increasing the number of the bells; and the pennies from clock-golf and treasure hunts have been turned into panelling and paint in the ringing chamber. These decorations will be simple, the panelling plain and the paint white, or buff; like a lighthouse which uses white paint inside to emphasise the brass lamp and glassy mirrors, the accent in the ringing chamber will be the coloured sallies, emphasised by the austere walls. There may be some peal boards, and photographs of ringers, a card from the Central Council on the maintenance of bells, perhaps, but no other ornament.

Above this room is the clock, with vanes that whirr round when it strikes; and above that again are the bells, dimly lit by the louvres, so that the wheels seem to rise up like those of a triumphal car submerged upon its back in a green and murky sea. The stairs go up from here to the door on to the roof; to pass through it you will generally need another key. Outside on the leads, the wind blows through the tracery and round the pinnacles, smacking the rope against the flag-pole, the church roof runs out to the east below, the gravestones are changed to edges underneath the tops of trees, and above your head the great gilded cock turns slowly to and fro.

The architects who developed the bell-tower had one constant problem—the force exerted on the masonry by the swinging bells. Small bells could be fitted into a cote, an extension of the wall above the line of the western or eastern gable—Radipole in Dorset has one for three bells —or in a turret, like those at Kings' Somborne in Hampshire, which has one of wood, and Burton Lazars in Leicestershire, which has one of stone. But cotes and little turrets could not be made strong enough to withstand the ringing of heavy bells.

The most primitive way of hanging these can be seen today at East Bergholt in Norfolk. The bells are not even put up in a tower, but the frame is raised above the ground and covered with a wooden roof. Another more elaborate version of this is at Brookland church on Romney Marsh in Kent, which has an octagonal bellhouse made of wood in the shape of three candle-snuffers placed one on top of the other. Some construction like these bell-houses and bell-cages may have held the three "most huge" bells at Glastonbury Abbey; eight more smaller ones were in the tower. Bishop Grandison in his statutes of 1339 for the government of the collegiate establishment at Ottery St. Mary in Devon, insisted that:

> "The ringing be not too long drawn out, and that it should not take place after the office or at dawn, as is the custom at Exeter, because 'a sounding brass and tinkling cymbal' are of no advantage to souls, and further, greatly harm the ears, the fabric and the bells."

At Ottery St. Mary a solemn Mass for the Virgin was sung in the Lady Chapel every day and before this Mass four special bells were rung according to whether the day was a special feast day, and:

> "the four larger bells aforesaid to hang as at Exeter on the right hand side of the church, the four other everyday ones on the left."

Dividing the bells between the two western towers of a church was one way of reducing the strain, and sometimes to prevent these taking a large part of the nave with them if they fell, they were contiguous but not tied to it. The distressing spectacle of the beautiful tower tumbling down to the sound of clanging bells, with stones and beams, and legs and arms tossed out all over the church could also be avoided if the bells were hung in an isolated tower of immense strength. In England these were called clochards, but now the Italian word campanile is more usual.

Chichester is the only English Cathedral with a surviving detached campanile; the one at Salisbury was taken down by Wyatt in 1789. This was constructed on the most massive scale; the interior of the tower was thirty-three feet square and the walls were eight feet thick, this stone part was eighty feet high to the top of the parapet. The ringing chamber was thirty-seven feet above the ground, and the belfry thirty-two feet above this. Rising up from the stone work, an octagonal battlemented lantern had a lead-covered spire rising from it, and on top of that a cross and a weathercock; the whole building was about two hundred feet high. The campanile and the bells were the victims of negligence; from 1740 they could not be rung in peal because of the dilapidated state of the frame. In 1777 numbers two, three, five, seven, and eight, which were all cracked, were sold at ten and sixpence a stone, and in 1793 number six was hung in the central tower of the Cathedral, and the treble and number four sold for a hundred and five pounds.

Thickness is everything today, guides always know the thickness of walls and show it with outstretched arms, and pause for the party to wonder. Even Stow was impressed by the thickness of the walls of Edward III's clochard in the Little Sanctuary at Westminster, whose three great bells "man fabled that their ringing sowred all the drink in the towne". Later the tower became a pub called the "Three Tuns". The squire of Llanfechell, Angle-

123

sea, in the eighteenth century felt the same relation between his beer and the church bells, and so fitted a device to the tower to decrease the vibration.

There are other detached towers in the country, particularly in East Anglia, Bedfordshire, and Cambridgeshire, but all are smaller than the one at Chichester. One theory is that they were refuge towers converted into belltowers, and this would seem to be reasonable of the ones at Marston Moretaine and at Elstow in Bedfordshire. There is a late-nineteenth-century one at Woburn Sands, but it is connected by a porch to the church. St. Mary's Sutton in Lincolnshire is another tower which to all intents is isolated, being attached to the church by the most tenuous stone thread.

The run of parish church towers are square and at the west end of the nave, but some are circular, or octagonal, with and without spires, with small flèches rising from their roofs, or bulky wooden steeples. Decoration has crept up them till it has reached the top, and the finest bell-towers, such as Boston Stump, rise up quite plain, till they burst into a froth of Gothic ornament. This is the basic principle of tower design, and one followed by Wren in his fifty-two variations on the theme of tower or spire. At Halifax it influenced the designers of the factory chimneys; anyone standing looking over this wonderful city from the Bradford road will see how the very square church tower with its restrained ornament on the parapet has influenced the chimneys which have iron crowns round their lips.

The later history of bell-towers is found in the development of the nineteenth-century commemorative clocktower. The architects who designed these borrowed styles from all Europe, chiefly Germany, so that the chance of confusion between Victoria's Jubilee clock and the church are small. At Berwick-on-Tweed, though, which has a church built during the Commonwealth with no tower or bells, the bells in the Town Hall ring for the service, and the Town Hall is so like a church that a regiment which was once quartered here marched to it to hear the service one Sunday, and on another occasion a visiting preacher was found hammering at its doors.

But as it is impossible to start a discussion of the commemorative clock, so it is impossible to go into the design of bell-towers in any greater detail. The things to look out for are cotes, turrets, cages, bell houses, isolated bell-towers, and anything else likely to catch the eye. A thousand other things will be found, from an eighteenth-century wooden cupola for a stable bell to the woggiest extravaganzas in cast-iron commemorating the termination of the Zulu War. Of the books on the subject, E. T. Green's *Towers and Spires, their Design and Arrangement,* while discussing British towers, does not limit its scope to Britain. A more specialised book is F. J. Allen's *The Great Church Towers of England.* This started as a study of the Somerset towers, and spread out to include all the types found in England; it is very well illustrated with photographs. In 1859 Charles Wickes published *The Spires and Towers of the Medieval Churches of England,* in three volumes, consisting of an introductory essay in each one followed by his drawings reproduced by lithography. These are both edifying and charming, even if they make every church look as if it had just been designed and built by Sir George Gilbert Scott, they provide valuable information on life in the nineteenth-century churchyard. If the church was in the town, a volunteer might be riding by, while towsers fight and snarl in the road, and old gentlemen peer at shop-girls through bubbly panes of glass. In the country, milkmaids carry wooden tubs on their heads, and goats and sheep nibble round the graves.

7

Belling the Cat

CHURCH bells, though they now make their own mathematical music, were originally intended as warnings and reminders, and bells used in other contexts have either become musical or remain shrill and minatory, telling us that we are about to be run over or are late. Besides the infinity of applications of the ordinary bell as a disturber of life, there is another kind used in less irritating ways: the bell which hangs on a jester's cap or round a ferret's neck, the crotal, a hollow metal sphere, containing a metal ball for a clapper. Many uses of crotals and bells; by butchers, candlestick makers, robe makers, and soap boilers from the earliest time have their origin shrouded with a convenient obscurity; and there is no need to enumerate them all, but only to take a few and those the ones which obtrude most sharply; and for a beginning, one which can be traced with some precision for the whole course of its history—the bicycle bell.

The golden age of the bicycle bell was from 1877 to

126

1900. Shining in its infancy, it rang on penny farthings and safeties which, with the horse and the steam traction-engine, alone competed for mastery of the road. Nowadays the merry tinkle is more rarely heard. It is useless for the cyclist to challenge a car, and he can only bully pedestrians, with whom he can be as peremptory today as a boy of the eighties who, after reading Cassell's *Book of Sports and Pastimes,* rode a Carver, a Hillman and Herbert, or a Surrey Invincible. For such a boy had learnt the hard way, and now, trailing behind him a plume of chalky dust, could hold his head proudly as he looked above the hedge tops, taller than any equestrian, controlling the first and last machine to dignify its rider.

As a tyro he had selected a penny farthing which was light, yet strong, and on the first day had taken it to some secluded spot and, sitting on the saddle but without putting his feet on the pedals, had tried to guide it down a gently sloping hill, "when the difficulty in maintaining balance will be immediately apparent". When he could balance he began to use the pedals and later learnt to dismount—"The machine running at a gentle pace, the rider takes both feet off the pedals and looking back under his left arm reaches his leg cautiously towards the step, taking care to avoid putting it into the wheel. Having got safely on the step he should rise on it, and lower himself until his other foot just touches the ground when he may drop with the hind wheel between his legs, having taken the precaution of seeing that it is not high enough to hurt him." But this is only a tyro's way of dismounting; the most fashionable method was to—"Dismount by a Vault. This when properly learnt is the best of all dismounts, as it is of service in any emergency. It consists simply in vaulting from the saddle by throwing one leg sharply backwards over the backbone, as in dismounting by the pedal. The rider should keep upright and throw only a little weight on the handles. You will get an idea of the proper position if you suppose that someone has grasped the backbone, and you wish to hack his hand with your heel. Carefully practised, it is the best of all methods." Hacking is the essence of the book; a large part of it is devoted to the cultivation of the chest, and even the handles of a bicycle should be held with the back of the hand downwards as this will throw out the chest, and hollow the back, the other prime object of late nineteenth-century body building. The part dealing with bicycling is illustrated with charming cuts of youths in knickerbockers and pill-box caps cycling unhappily downhill with their legs over the handlebars, while their brothers on other pages play cricket, footer, ride, swim, fence, skate or slide—"The boy who has never in his early days enjoyed a good slide is never very likely to enjoy any manly outdoor exercise."

Bicycling was one of the gentler sports, for the more reserved boys. They are all melancholy as they hack the backbone or spring lightly off the step, and the details of their stockinged legs and shoes, giving the position of the foot when "testing for reach" or "driving", are most clerically black and dim. Certainly they must have been the children of an impoverished country clergyman who could not afford bicycles with the fashionable red tyres. Even when they went touring they were not able to follow the instruction that "for head-gear, a well-ventilated helmet, with plenty of brim back and front, is undoubtedly the best, though not so natty-looking as a polo cap". For them always their elder brothers'—now in some Colonial police force—cast-off pill-box. They could never enjoy the pleasure of streaming along in the well-ordered ranks of some chic cycling club, ears pricked for the thrilling call of the bugle signalling to their captain in the van that their vice-captain or adjutant has had to fall out and deal with some scratched, bleeding body who was foolish enough to have a cheap light hanging from his hub, and which has thrown him off by blocking the wheel. "Next to a cheap and nasty machine, nothing is so dangerous as a cheap and badly-constructed lamp." The sad boys' bells, too, were of a simple kind, not for them "the 'Arab' actuated by the spokes, giving some 1,500 strokes per minute", but the simple dog-bell. What they were good at, though, was the conduct of the bicycle with the horse. "When riding should he unfortunately meet a restive horse, and should the animal show signs of fright when far away, the cyclist should immediately dismount, and, having put the machine out of sight, should offer to lead the animal by. If, on the other hand, the horse should shy when close to the rider, the latter should spurt rapidly by, as if he dismounts, the sudden motion and noise would frighten the animal still more." These earnest boys never tore past governess carts with the "Arab" going full blast.

At first it was felt that a bicycle was such a dangerous machine that the bell should ring all the time, so a large crotal was hung from the handle, perhaps it was Challis's cycle bell, the "loudest, best finished and most desirable bell". In 1881 Challis introduced his stop-bell, similar to the other but with the ball on a chain so that it could be pulled up and held tightly to the side of the crotal, when it would not ring however much it was vibrated. In August 1881 a leader in the *Cyclist* said that the continuously ringing bell was quite useless, as the noise was so familiar that no one noticed a bicycle bell when they heard it. Many people invented loud and startling bells of the most dazzling ingenuity. They were built into the handles so that a twist or a push sounded them, or, like the Arab, were struck by the spokes of the front wheel, or they rang as soon as the brakes were applied or directly a certain speed was reached. There were special bells operated by strong springs which could be released with terrific noise 'f the cyclist was attacked by a dog, for on a penny farthing it was difficult to give that hack to the teeth which is possible from the lower seat of a safety. Electric dynamos operated lamps and bells, and a horn and bell were combined so that when a lever was pressed it blew the horn and if pressed down still farther rang a bell. In 1898, S. Bündel invented a mechanism for blowing a horn on a bicycle—the space between the saddle, handlebars, and pedals was filled with a cylinder, a horn, and an air pump, worked by a piston from the pedals. When the rider pressed a button the air was released from the cylinder and blew the horn. Wind was also used for a more luxurious warning system; a rider who liked to smoke could buy a pipe or cigar-holder so constructed that when he blew down it he made a tiny crotal ring; but the difficulties of this device were insuperable, the intricate valves and bell gear, all on so miniature a scale, became clogged with thick nicotine, and at the moment when a tinkle would save an old lady a nasty fright, the cigar-holder alarm was silenced by the dottley sludge. In 1911, Lucas's patented the mechanism which rang two bells at the same time. This became very popular with errand-boys who would flash round corners, empty baskets hung round their necks, whistling tunes from the latest musical comedy, and ringing the bells on their bicycles. The last war though, gave youth opportunities for earning more money more easily, and the only errand-boys one sees now are very old men, who whistled *The Chocolate Soldier* at the beginning of their careers and, never rising higher, still thinly whistle tunes from naughty operettas, being unable to shape their old lips round the "bop bop beebudy bop" which those who should be doing their job whistle as they spray oil over the upholstery of motor-cars.

At the beginning of this century the bicycle bell was perfected, and the inventors were lucky to find that the motor-car, which at first promised to make enough noise to warn anybody of its approach, was becoming more silent. In no time they were patenting bells and horns which were worked by the exhaust gases, sirens, bells hanging on springs from the chassis ringing continuously when the car was stolen, rattles, horns worked by hydraulics and compressed air. At last the horn, either electric or pneumatic, was established as the best and noisiest, and the inventors

turned to the problem of amplifying recorded sound. The
Metropolitan Police, to distinguish their patrol cars from
others, fitted electric bells in 1933, and their quick
mechanical beat is distinct from the fire-engine or tram.

Hewitt and Rhodes' model code of rules for a municipal
or private tramway gives instructions for the use of the
bell. After he has drawn from the store his insulated glove,
and the beautiful brass keys like frozen swans' necks which
he twirls throughout the day, the driver must see that he
has a bell tramp. This he must sound sharply before starting
the car, when passing a side street, turning the corners,
when vehicles are in front, and when passing another car.
There was also a code using the conductor's bell at each
end of the car as a signal between the driver and the conductor. From the conductor to the driver, one ring meant
stop; two, start; three, stop quickly; and four, car full, so
fly past the request stops; driver to conductor signals were:
one ring, throw in automatic switch; two, attend to trolley;
and three, come and speak.

Hewitt and Rhodes published their book in 1902; in
1904 the *Fire Call* for December 6th reported that at a
meeting of the L.C.C. £84 was sanctioned for the purchase
of bells to be fixed to the engines so that people would be
warned to get out of the way. Before this firemen called
out "Hi Hi Hi" in the same rhythm as the ringing bells
today. A month later the *Fire Call* announced that the
L.C.C. were determined to adopt bells—"The gong will
not be an exclusive possession of the fireman who will
have to share it with motors and electric cars." The London
Fire Brigade were later than others in adopting the bell.
Many provincial fire brigades used them years before, and
a music cover by Concannon of the "Fire Brigade Galop",
published in 1863 (dedicated to Captain Frederick Hodges,
the renowned fire-fighter, by Lieutenant Becker of Hodges
Fire Brigade and the Volunteer Fire Brigades of England),
shows two horse-drawn engines "The Deluge" and "The
Torrent", both made by Merryweathers and each with a

great bell. Merryweathers' catalogue for 1882 has a fine wood engraving of their patent double-cylinder steam fire-engine "Cachapoal", made for the Valparaiso Brigade. It was very similar to the "Torrent" and the "Deluge", and carried a bell. This firm still manufactures fire-engines and casts bells for them; and before the last war they had in their catalogues various carillon bells for giving the alarm; there was the "Utrimque", which hung beneath a trim canopy of zinc to protect it in inclement weather; the "Utro", two bells joined together, that made a clashing noise which could not be confused with the factory bell; the "Usucapio" was struck by a clock-work hammer operated by weights. Fire engines can either have a mechanical bell or one struck by hand, which is the best method, louder and more distinctive, urging other traffic to the side of the road and encouraging the drivers.

Before the fine time when we could move about on bicycles and in motor-cars, life on the roads was accompanied by the continual sound of bells. Occasionally one still finds a cow bonking about on a moor or a marsh with a bell round its neck; sheep and goats also, their bells hanging from a wooden yoke. The cow may have the same kind of harness, though generally the bell hangs from a plain leather strap.

A herd of cows whose leader wears a bell grazes on the road from Romsey to Winchester, where it crosses a dreary plain of gorse bushes and heather, and in Winchester Cathedral is the tomb of Sir Arnald de Gaveston, who lies on his back in the retro-choir beside putrefying *memento-mori* bishops, their bones appearing through the tightened skin. Sir Arnald carries his shield at his left side, and his arms include three grazing cows, one above another, with bells hanging from their necks, like the cow on the road; a more unpleasant *memento mori* than the bishops.

But where bells are concerned the horse has always been the thing. Pack-horses and the horses of teams pulling

wagons had bells on their harness. The leader of a string
of pack-horses would have the bells or crotals sewn to its
bridle, and, like the bell mare used by the gaucho, it would
lead the others behind it. Wagon teams, too, carried
bells to give warning of their approach, particularly if they
were in a deep and twisting lane. They would have them
hanging from an arch of wood covered with a worsted
fringe held in place by brass-headed nails. Perhaps only
one horse would carry these, or each horse would carry
some, like those described by Hardy in *The Woodlanders*,
where each horse had four bells, the four sets making two
octaves, jingling constantly with the slow and ponderous
movement. Each farmer would have his own series of
bells on his teams, so that they could be recognised by their
ringing when heard round a corner in the daytime or at
night, in the same way that boatmen on the canals know
who it is directly they hear the note of another engine
coming towards them on the cut.

Smarter bell-terrets are shown in the saddlers' catalogues
of the nineteenth century, printed in yellow to show their
brassiness and arranged symmetrically on the page. The
largest are for five bells, but two or three seems to have been
the most popular number. Some are ordinary bells, and
others crotals; from one terret of three a tall tuft of hair
shoots up like a rocket above the horse's back, and the
smartest of them bear their owner's crest—pelicans in their
piety or "Marquesses' Coronets without cushions". These
are all for cart harness. The devotees of the carriage horse
and hunter never took to bells, and produced for their
horses the most restrained and functional harness; a little
quiet silver was allowed for carriages, but the true delight
was, and still is, the contrast of rich textures, pigskin, hide
or patent leather against that glossy polished coat; appre-
ciation undisturbed by the embellishment of bells. Even
coster harness, with its special straps and circles of coloured
patent, never used them, and they are reserved for the
cart-horse, large enough to take everything, bells, braid,

and brass. The noise of bells is always associated with two horse-drawn vehicles, the cab and the sleigh; the latter evoking vistas of conifers and larches, serfs, snow, weddings, and a furry womb of sables for two.[1]

The bell which still rings in some parts of the country as a survivor of the morning bell and curfew, is the estate bell, whose sound begins work in the morning, stops it at lunch, and finishes it again in the evening. The factory bell, now similarly obsolescent, rang more often starting work and stopping it for all the breaks for snacks. At Chatham Dockyard one of the bells rang under a small lead-covered canopy, on top of a tall pole like a bear's pole, by the Dockyard gate. This use of a bell as a signal to start and stop an action is so common that once the train of thought has started, the mind becomes bogged with examples in a few moments and also with the idea of the bell as a warning and as an indication; its use at boxing matches, and by bus conductors, its ringing in cash registers and on those old overhead railways in draper's shops which took money to the cash desk. At ferries one sometimes rings a bell to summon a man in a rowing-boat. In winter, there were muffin-men; and coaches which used to be started from their termini by the ringing of a bell. Coaches evoke their own picturesque of four-in-hand events at agricultural shows, clean and gleaming, the hard reality; and their commoner appearance at Christmas on our mantelpieces axle-deep in snow, the guard straining at the spokes of the wheel, while the passengers huddle together, a dim church in the distance, lantern light, and robins. Fortunately this aspect of Christmas is becoming more popular again, putting the Vermeers, the home-designed, and the witty back into their place. With the stage-coach comes another figure of contemporary folk-lore, the kindly old bellman—not the one in *The Hunting of the Snark*—in a many-caped coat, carrying a lantern, and a bell, to bring you every good wish and prosperity for

[1] See Appendix A.

134

Christmas from the So-and-So's, also a Happy New Year; a reminder that there are two festivals to try our stomachs in a week.

The year 1556 is a common date for the institution of bellmen but there are references to them before this. The Guild of Holy Cross in Birmingham let a house free to the bellman in return for service which he gave to the Guild; and at Lancaster in 1377 members of the Guild of Holy Trinity were to attend *placebos* and *diriges* if summoned by him or pay a fine of two-pence. The frontispiece to Dekker's *Belman of London* is a cut of a bellman walking along with a dog at his heels; over his shoulder he carries a pike, and in one hand a lantern, while in the other is a bell to give warning in case of fire; he has a somewhat sullen and morose expression. An underpaid and corruptible police force, the bellmen were more often than not deliberately incompetent; if they apprehended a thief entering a house or a prostitute plying her trade on a street corner, they were only too willing to accept bribes for not taking them to the watch-house.

Part of a bellman's duty, as everyone knows, was to call out the hour and the state of the weather, often he would end his chant with this exhortation: "Take care of your fire and candle, be charitable to the poor and pray for the dead"; and sometimes he would end a proclamation with "God Save the King and the Lord of this Manor". His yelling at all hours of the night was considered a great bore, but it was at Christmas that he really started to make a nuisance of himself. Like the gas-lamp lighters in the nineteenth century who wrote poems and then sold them to the houses in the street whose lamps they lit, the bellman would do the same thing, producing terrible doggerel, like this piece of a poem written by Mr. Gutheridge, Bellman and Beadle of St. Leonard's, Shoreditch.

To look askew upon the church by some is deem'd a crime
But all must do it at Shoreditch church, all who would
*   know the time.*

135

The figures on the dial plate 45678,
Being hid behind the pediment, if you look at it straight,
The brains sure of the architect must in confusion been
When he five figures of the twelve prevented being seen.

Towards the end of the eighteenth century they were generally abhorred both for the noise they made at night, for their Christmas poems, and for the fact that they were not an efficient guard against burglary. In 1770 *The Mobiad or Battle of the Voice,* by Democritus Juvenal, published in Exeter, described them thus:

Next Beadles (as in packs of cards be knaves
Two couple just) with brazen headed staves
In tuck'd blue vests, and bonnets gold of brim
(What Turks Head sign stares tho moustached so grim)
The staves they bear
Not those which in black winter nights they knock
From rest us startle—but to learn the Clock
Or feel tremendous rhyme in mumbling wise
Croak'd horrible, our tingling ears chastise
When dismal voice, and dismal clink of bell
Inflict good morrow, with Death Judgement Hell.

Bellmen must have been very like those men diseased by the tedium of their occupations one sometimes meets in offices, car-parks, and museums, who in reply to a perfectly civil question put up a flat yellow hand and say, "No, No, No, I am afraid the answer's No", before one has even finished speaking or they have comprehended the query. At the end of the eighteenth century bellmen went round the streets each evening before the receiving houses for the mails closed, collecting the letters for a small fee; finally the postmen took this job over.

If the bellman's bell made life noisy in the street at night, similar, smaller bells have dominated life indoors. In the Ashmolean and the Victoria and Albert Museums are the small silver bells of the eighteenth century, made perhaps to stand singly on the table, or as part of a standish, elegantly polished; one rang, and a servant appeared. A hundred years later the inventors of table bells were bombarding the Patent Office with their specifications. One of the first improvements was to incorporate the bell into a match-stand, another device was to incorporate a bell into a vessel for iced water; it had a receptacle for matches and a flower vase, and the head of the delivery pump had a bell push fitted to it. In 1902 M. Berhnhardt patented an electrically operated cigar lighter, cigar cutter, ash-tray, and bell; advertisements or pictures could be put into a frame at the side, and the top could be used as a money-box. In the year of Edward VII's Coronation there was a crown-shaped table bell; then there was a combined cigar cutter, match-box, snuff-box, ash-tray, and gong; bells in the form of ginger-beer bottles; a call bell which incorporated a tumbler for toothpicks. Smokers' combination articles, as they were called, always included a bell; some were hidden in flower-stands, or just plainly stood on top of the ash-tray or match-holder, for this was the age of the waiter and the b and s.

If one went to the seaside in the early years of this century, on a ringing tour perhaps, on one's bedroom door there might have been a machine like a ship's telegraph. After a session in the nearest Palm Lounge discussing ropes or grandsire, ringing the call-bell concealed in the tooth-pick receptacle and perhaps even listening to some recorded music played by a machine artfully concealed in a plant stand, you went upstairs to bed feeling a trifle peckish. The telegraph on your door caught your eye, and you looked at it carefully for the first time. In fact there were two dials, the upper one was a clock which, once set inside, showed the same time on another dial on the outside of the door, so that the chambermaid could come and ring a bell inside your room at whatever time you wished to be called in the morning. The lower dial was marked out in a series of requests. As you were hungry you spun the dial round to fish and rang a bell; then selected any other dishes you wanted for a light supper, eggs, champagne, and coffee. On really elaborate installations·the dial on your door had a corresponding one in the kitchen downstairs, repeating your signals electrically. Up came your meal, and if afterwards you felt slightly off colour, a b and s. would soon settle that, so up you got and dialled again; but the b and s only made you worse, so you selected cocoa, milk, seltzer or tea, and finally asked for the doctor, all without stirring from your room. It was a pity that this system never became popular, for it cuts out the telephone and limits the range of disappointment; certainly one would never think of asking for asparagus for breakfast if it were not marked on the dial. But one could be sure that everything except tea would be off, and that the handle would stick despairingly at champagne.

Today the Palm Lounge is no more, and in the place of the combination article we have the crinolined lady, of rough brass, a posy in one hand, her body, head, and bonnet forming a handle and a clapper concealed beneath her skirts, tinkling for a pot of tea for two, toast, scones, and cakes. She is a cheap descendant from the table bells by Paul Lamerie, and between the two in time is the Pussy. She, poor soul, should have a tiny crotal, or ferret's bell, or hawk's bell round her neck, as she stares at the little girls with the blue sash in the Christmas number supplement, or frolics in the garden with a puppy chum. Whiskers, that cat who was mentioned in chapter one, has a bell round her neck, but as she is in black and white one cannot tell the colour of the ribbon. Some people consider it bad form to bell the cat, and say that Snowballs, Tinkers, Stripes, and Fluffs will hang themselves upon the little straps or ribbons round their necks. One cat which will never hang itself is the fat ginger podge who patrols the forecourt of the British Museum. On winter days, if it is not raining, he lies on the warm radiators of cars, and in the summer on the hot metal roof of a saloon or the hammock-like canvas of a hood. This cat has a little brass bell

138

round his neck hanging from a thin leather strap, and sometimes, like the older scholars, he looks up and sees the grass, the duffle-coats, and cameras.

Other things than the cat have worn crotals or hawk's bells. In 1585 the Recorder of London wrote this to Lord Burleigh:

"Amongst our travels this one matter tumbled out by the way. One Wootton, a gentleman born, and some time a merchant of good credit, having fallen by time, into decay, kept an ale house at Smart's Key near Billingsgate; and after for some misdemeanour, being put down, he reared up a new trade of life, and in the same house he procured all the cut purses about this city to repair to this said house. There was a school-house set up to learn young boys to cut purses. There were hung up two devices: the one was a pocket, the other was a purse. The pocket had in it certain counters, and was hung about with hawk's bells and over the top did hang a little sacring bell; and he that could take out a counter without any noise was allowed to be a public hoyster, and he that could take a piece of silver out of the purse without the noise of any of the bells he was adjudged a judicial nipper. N.B. That a hoyster is a pickpocket and a nipper is termed a pickpurse or a cut purse."

This picture of a thieves' school takes one farther back in time, and back still farther to the Middle Ages to jongleurs and jesters, presumably looking as they do at pageants today, with their horned caps and bells, and to the jingling of bells at festivals and dances. At Congleton, on the Feast of St. Peter ad Vincula, the patronal festival, boys ran through the streets at midnight wearing belts covered with bells whose noise was supposed to represent the clanking of St. Peter's chains, now safely stored in St. Peter ad Vincula in Rome, and shown to the faithful by pressing a button, which rolls back with cinema-organ smoothness the sliding doors of the reliquary.

Today the boys of Congleton are brought to mind by Morris Dancers. One of the great days in the year is May morning at Oxford; after the clock has struck and the hymn

139

been sung on Magdalen Tower the Oxford University Morris Men parade up the street to the Radcliffe Camera and dance there. Sensibly they wear straw hats decorated with flowers, not cricket caps, which are allowed by Sharpe but which look ridiculous; and for the "Haste to the Wedding", "How d'ye do, Sirs", "Old Mother Oxford", and "Old Woman Tossed Up in a Blanket", whichever of these dances they perform, they have strapped to their legs "ruggles" or garters. These are pads sewn all over with rosettes of coloured ribbon and little bells. At Bampton they have pieces of rag, like a rag rug, between the bells instead of ribbons; but however gay they are, they still look like patches of some mandrilline disease on the dancers' legs. Their purpose is that when the dancers Caper Out, Shake-up, Straddle Clip, Fore-caper, and Once to Yourself, the bells shall ring as their bent legs are waved above the ground.

But the Hawk, as one of the originators of small bells, now hardly wears them, for so few are trained. The trouble with hawk's bells is that, attached as they are to the birds' legs by leather "bewits", they are always getting dented on the block of wood the bird stands on, and so lose their tone.

Dame Juliana Berners said that a hawk's bells should be exactly matched for weight and be of a good shrill sound, and that one should be a semitone lower than the other. The best of them came from Dordrecht. Cox's *Gentleman's Recreation* tells one how to train and fly hawks, but except for the sculpture at the beginning of this section, which displays the equipment used, there is no great detail on the bells, for their sole use is to enable the falconer to trace the bird when it is out of sight. It is a fascinating book. Cox gives one a select list of names for hounds and beagles "for the convenience of a young gentleman as may in time keep a kennel"—Banger, Fuddle, Lillups, Mopsie, Singwel and Truelips are five of them, and there are such resounding sentences as this.

"Since the dissolution and spoil of Paradise, no man hath either seen, or can give the names of all land-Fowl whatever, there being such great variety, every country producing some particular sorts, which are unknown to other nations."

He describes the use of dead engines:

"Some there are that stalk with stags or Red-deer form'd out of painted canvas, with the natural horns of stags fixt theron, and the colour so lively painted that the fowl cannot discern the fallacy; and these are very useful in low fenny grounds, where any such deer do usually feed, and are more familiar with the fowl, and so feed nearer them than Ox, Horse or Cow."

Some gentlemen preferred stalking behind painted trees or an interwoven screen of bushes. But this was for shooting birds, and since:

"According to the judgement of most men the nightingale carries the bell from all other singing birds, opening her charming mouth not only sweetly but with much variety of pleasant notes"

there is a great deal of instruction in the taking of birds alive.

In plain and champaign countries between the end of October and the end of March, one went Low Belling at night. The bell must have a deep and hollow sound, and the air be mild, with moonshine. The hunters walk into a stubble-field, behind the man with the bell, carrying a net at the corners and sides; in their free hands they have links or bundles of straw, and behind is another man bearing an iron or stone vessel containing burning but not blazing coals.

"The sound of the bell makes the birds lie close for the sound is dreadful to them but when the net is pitched and bundles of straw which you carry or links are lit at the coals they will be terrified and fly into the net."

141

After one netful the party moved on in darkness behind the melancholy bell till they had pitched their net again.

Another technique, though not with a bell, was for catching birds which roosted in shrubs and bushes; again men went out with lights, which they held round the bushes and making a noise the birds flew out to be so amazed by all the light and din that they hovered in the air and allowed themselves to be beaten down to the ground by "long poles with great bushy tops fixed to them".

Hand-bells and crotals have rattled and rung round these islands for many centuries, and today the bell-buoys of Trinity House ring in the channels and estuaries, out from the land, though on shore one hears bells less frequently than a hundred years ago. Nowadays more people can read, and with electricity we can have an illuminated sign saying Northern Line, Edgware Train. But think what it would be like if a man had to give an intricate number of strokes on a handbell as well as trying to yell the train at the top of his voice. Clearly, though, we like noise, for if increased literacy has been the end of the folk arts, the ballads, and the bells, it has also accompanied a significant and presumably pleasing increase in din. So much so that with the exception of those people who live near an airfield or a race-track, the noise of a jet plane or a Bugatti comes as a welcome variant in the background rumble which marks life in a town.

8

Bells for Skulls and Markets

THE first electric bell I knew was derelict and lay in two parts in a cupboard under a flight of stairs. One was a mahogany box made to hang on the wall. In it were two porcelain pots, with rods in them and a deposit of white dust; later I learnt that this was a Leclanché cell. Twisted wires, insulated with silk the colour of green sunshades, went to the bell, which was fixed on a slab of mahogany; the coils and magnets, tremblers and points were cased in with still more polished mahogany. I never heard this bell, for the bells in that house were rung by pulling wires.

At one time the front door bell, which rang with a deafening clang just inside the porch above one's head, was felt to be ringing in the wrong place and miles of copper wire were taken up into the roof, round corners on bell-cranks, down through the floors, and into the walls to a bell by the back door. But the strongest pull[1] on the bell-

¹ See Appendix B.

pull at the front door only took up a small length of the miles of slack wire and so made no sound. Then a new electric bell was installed, which worked wonderfully until the ingenious Meccano contact on the old bellpush rusted. Now the loud bell in the porch is used again and everybody is satisfied.

Generally though, the electric bell has replaced those which hung on coiled springs in the outbacks of houses. Many of these must have been installed in the late eighteenth or early nineteenth century, for it was then that the system of springs, wire, and cranks was perfected, and bell-hangers could advertise that they hung alarms on a new and improved construction, or that they could install them without damaging stucco or painting. After Faraday's discovery of the electro-magnet more wires were led round the skirting boards, and the art of the embroidered and beaded bell-pull died as steadily as its contemporary, the smoking-cap. One of the first discoveries made by the electricians fitting these new bells was that if the old type of pull was turned into a switch, anyone conditioned to them would give such a great tug that it was invariably broken. So the button became the most popular way of ringing the bell—though that phrase would seem to refer to the bells on "try your strength" machines at fairs and not to house bells—and for really high-class work these were sunk in little square wooden boxes in the wall, and then covered with an artistic plate, painted with pansies or a nice full-blown rose. In our century the bell-push in modest yet refined homes is often hidden under the carpet at one end of the dining-table or even screwed on to it, so that the hostess can unobtrusively summon a maid to change the plates. Complicated domestic electric bells have indicators to show in which room the button has been pushed. Some of the largest of these are in one of the tunnels at Welbeck Abbey. Each is about four feet square, the glass is painted a dark green and the little holes through which the wobbling tallies show are edged with gold.

144

Colleagues of the men who invented the bicycle bell were at the same time adapting the electric bell to many different purposes. The most common were burglar alarms; switches could be fixed on windows to ring bells if they were opened, and the locks on doors could be wired so that if the lock was picked or forced with a key, a bell would ring. Some of the others were to give warning of gas escaping from a meter; to ring a bell when an automatic candle-snuffer had put out the light; and to alarm a household if someone turned a door-knob. Not electric, but in the same class are a bright red crotal fixed to a cork for a poison bottle, and a patent taken out in 1893 for a luminous bell-push. If one was sufficiently dexterous to fix special con-tacts on to the hands of an ordinary clock, it could be made to ring an electric bell, and the clock with a little alteration could serve as the fuse of a time-bomb.

The railway companies have used electric bells since the 1840s, and handbells were so common on the railway, and so strident, that the saying "As harsh as a porter's bell" became a common simile. These were rung just before a train left or arrived at a station, were engraved with the company's name or initials, and stood on blocks of wood with a recess scooped out of the centre to take the flight of the clapper. A relic of this tradition is preserved on the District Line. The guard strokes two wires with the copper ferrule on the stick of his flag, which causes the bell to ring on the platform at the driver's end of the train, telling him to start. Failing to ring the bell was a serious offence. In June 1843, Sergeant Moore of the Great Western Rail-way was dismissed the service for falling asleep while on duty at Paddington, and failing to ring the bell for the arrival of the up train.

The G.W.R. also had large bells in station yards which the policeman on duty would ring to warn passengers that a train was due, and at the opening of Eastbourne Station in 1849, a specially engraved handbell rang to start the first train. Later, when the staff of the railways was organised into signalman, police, and porters, the porters would ring the bell; and when the practice was abandoned, one line superintendent on the L.M.S. collected a great number of bells, took off the clappers, and used them as aspidistra pots.

Bells on the rolling-stock of railways were less common. The Royal George, an engine designed by Hackworth in 1827, carried a large bell, and so did the G.W.R.'s George V, after its visit to America and Canada in 1937. On the G.W.R. in the 1880s a passenger who wished to stop the train could pull a cord which rang a bell fixed to the driver's side of the tender, and in 1900 a communication bell, again rung by pulling a cord, was fitted in the guard's-van. Passengers today have bells to summon the attendant in Pullman cars and first-class carriages. In the railway carriage which used to take her to Balmoral, Queen Victoria had buttons which rang bells with a peremptory ping, in the compartments occupied by John Brown and her ladies-in-waiting. Edward VII had the softest down cushions in the arm-chairs of his train, and a great many elegant white switches and buttons by his bedside, for turning on the fans, adjusting the temperature and ventilation, and for calling his valet and equerry.

Handbells were not widely used by the railways for signalling to the drivers of trains, though in 1847 the London and North-Western Railway printed this rule in their rule book.

> "In fog, when a train is going up Warrington Incline a bell is rung to give notice to the enginemen on the Liverpool and Manchester Railway that such is the case so that if necessary they may stop before coming to the crossing."

This was far too haphazard a warning and, for fog, bells were soon replaced by detonators which explode with a loud bang beneath the engine's wheels. But for signalling between signal-boxes bells are ideal; a code can easily be memorised, and the mechanism is as comparatively simple as any piece of railway-signalling equipment can be. At

146

first the signal-boxes were not joined with a telegraph, and only tunnels might be wired for signalling from one end to the other; the policeman on duty would signal when a train went in, and his mate at the other end would ring back when it came out. Nowadays when all railway signalling is performed to the liturgical ringing of small bells, as well as the wobbling of indicators, there is an exciting code for relaying news from one box to another. The London Brighton and South Coast Railway's rule book for 1909 included these signals in its code. Five rings equalled, back engines assisting in rear of goods train; nine, stop and examine train; ten, vehicles running away on right line.

Electric bells are so ubiquitous nowadays that it is not encouraging to think about them. They break up the day ringing in a telephone, they ring for hours outside shops when a burglar alarm goes wrong—the sound is so common in London that one wonders if they ever succeed in helping the police to catch a burglar; we have them in our homes, and they make visiting friends, who live in large Victorian houses divided into flats, hazardous when there is no light on all the buttons at the front door, and these are not nearly as efficient as the telephone things one sees in films of gangster life, in which the hero carefully carrying a corsage in a cellophane box presses a button and speaks to his bustylicious charmer before he floats up to her in the lift.

In a battleship the bell telling the time every half-hour throughout the watches is relayed through loudspeakers to all parts of the ship. In the seventeenth century the ship's bell hung beneath a carved and gilded canopy of wood, similar in intent, though different in style, to the canopy over the bell from Nelson's *Victory,* which still hangs in a shelter of carved wood representing anchors and ropes and dolphins, on the terrace of the destroyed Crystal Palace at Sydenham. The noise of ship's bells for the landsman is wrapped up with visions of steam and sail, mists on rivers, and the creak of rigging, and sailors using bells as fonts for the christening of their children, and of the Lutine Bell at Lloyd's, which was salvaged from the frigate *Lutine* in 1859, sixty years after she sank. The bell hangs in the underwriters room and is rung before the members are told important news, one stroke for bad, and two strokes for good, and never, as is commonly supposed, to announce the total loss of a vessel.

We can forget the grimmer side of life in sailing ships, described by Melville and Robert Hay, whose damp sleep in wet clothes was interrupted by the bell. The tedium on a sailing ship could be eased by knotting belts and lanyards for bells, and skrimshaw work, and in the concentration of the mind on misery or escape, but always the bell would be heard, saying that one watch was half done or that another was on its way. The most melancholy ringing of a ship's bell must have been when a ship foundered, and it rang with the motion of the waves, erratically and continually, intensifying the suffering of the sailors who clung to the rigging, like the crew of the brig *George*. This ship foundered and the crew, and one of their wives, Joice Rea, with her child, climbed to the main-top for safety; the child was the first to be washed away, and then Joice Rea died, but stayed tied to the mast with her husband and the other men. Soon they were suffering from thirst, as they had no fresh water, and Rea was forced to join with other members of the crew in drinking his wife's blood and in eating her flesh. Only the captain and one seaman survived, being over twenty days in the main-top before they were rescued, and in that time they sustained themselves on the bodies of their friends.

The first spring-driven clocks small enough to be called watches still had bells like the large clocks from which they were developed. Their cases were elaborately worked and the necessity for a grille to let out the sound of the bell was an opportunity for an intricate design in filigree,

148

which could be continued lightly chased on the gold or
silver case. Even if the watch was the size of a cricket ball
and did not keep accurate time, it was a pretty and
delicate piece of jewellery.

The designer of sixteenth-century watches worked in
an age morbidly conscious of time and death, and
sympathised with such wonderful nonsense as Donne's
"Methusalem, with all his hundreds of years was but a
mushroom of a night's growth, to this Day". The watch-
makers, taking a line from the poets and their patrons,
found the skeleton figure with his hour-glass and scythe
their inspiration. Mary Queen of Scots had a watch in the
shape of a skull, silver gilt. The cranium was divided into
four areas decorated with pictures and texts. Death with
his scythe and glass were engraved on the forehead, one
foot pointing to a palace, the other to a cottage, and as
a border round him were the lines from Horace's first
book of odes: "Pallida Mors aequo pulsat pede
pauperum tabernas Regumque turres." Above the left
ear, Adam stood beside the Tree of Knowledge with Eve
and the serpent, while a squirrel brisked about in the
grass. "Peccando perditionem miseriam aeternam posteris
memeri" divided this side of the head from the other;
above the right ear was the crucifixion of Christ between
the two thieves, and "Sic justitia mortem superavit,
salutem comparavit". The back of the head showed time
devouring all things, with another quotation from
Horace: "Tempus edax rerum tuque invidiosa vetustas."

Below the pictures and their mottoes, on a line running
right round the head from the angle of the lower jaw on
one side to the same point on the other, was a band of
filigree of crosses and foliage to allow the sound of the bell
to escape; other emblems of the Passion were worked into
this design—nails, scourges, thongs, a crown of thorns,
lanterns, hammers, pincers, ladders and also the text "Scala
cœli ad gloriam via". To tell the time the skull was turned
upside down (it would lie comfortably in the palm of the

hand) and the lower jaw lifted up, which took with it a piece of silver which can be described as the bottom of the brain-pan; this disclosed the dial in the roof of the mouth. On the inside of the lid was a picture of the stable at Bethlehem and the text "Gloria in Excelsis Deo, et in terra pax hominibus bona volu". The works naturally occupied the brain-pan, and there was a small silver bell for striking the hours. On the top of the skull a chain was fixed to a staple to allow the watch to be carried about.

Bells were fitted in watches for the next three hundred years. But now watches are worn on the wrist, either aggressively masculine, with knobs and dials to tell how long ago one took off from land and at what time one will touch it again, or over-feminine, "my lady's dainty wrist watch" of fiction, so no one carries a repeating, chiming watch with a case in dog-winkle stripes, and a bus load of workers from the city in the evening is not the tinkling cymbal it could be at the hours and quarters.

The obvious connection of time, death, and clocks was not missed by William Bowyer, who made a lantern clock in 1623 with the figure of death, and this verse inscribed on the flat surface of the doors:

> Man is a glase, life
> Is as water weakly washed about
> Sinne brought in Death.
> Death breakes the glase
> So runnes this water out.

The bells in these lantern clocks were seldom engraved, which seems strange in an age which so admired the elaboration of plain surfaces with flat patterns.

The bell has a thin time in the history of English clock making. In elaborate musical clocks, with eight or more hemispherical bells contained one inside the other like a nest of boxes, they could play tunes and sound nicely, hidden in elegant confections of inlay and metalwork or homely coffins of plain wood. Clockmakers have never made bells into a decorative feature; sometimes the Chinese taste allowed a mandarin to have a rendezvous with time in a bamboo pavilion on top of the case, but never did any fashion use the bells which were played for the hours and quarters or for the tunes to appear as the breasts of Venus or the brass posteriors of Mars.

This is a sad decline, for the weight-driven clock was invented solely to tell a man when to ring the bell for the canonical hours in the monastery or the hours of day and night in the town. In England these clocks, when they had been adapted to ring the bells, as well as tell the time, were almost always in a church tower; for the bells were there for them to ring, using one stroke to represent a unit; it took the ingenious seventeenth-century mind of Joseph Knibb to invent a striking mechanism which struck the Roman numerals. One small bell represented the unit and a large one the five, so that eight o'clock would sound as one blow on the large bell followed by three on the small one.

As the bell was a familiar signal and because few people could read, many of the first church clocks had no face on the outside of the tower. Some of these survive and Oxford is a good place to see them—Merton, New College, Magdalen, and Christ Church belfries have clocks with no external face, merely chiming and striking the hours and quarters to indicate the time. At Crowcombe, a nice not too-thatched village on the south side of the Quantocks, the church tower was struck by lightning in 1735 and the face of the clock destroyed, since when they have used none other, the clock only striking the hours. A refinement on the clock with no face is the clock with a face but with only an hour hand; Westminster Abbey has one of these. Great Bardfield in Essex, Ickfield, and Weathersfield have clocks which strike a small bell on the outside of the tower, and so has the chapel of a preparatory school at Elstree. The school has moved and the chapel is now derelict. There is a clock on the north wall of the north transept, and the hour and quarter bells cast in 1907 hang from five brackets pierced with quatrefoils fixed to the red and black brick walls. Elder trees and grass grow in the gutters, and the south side of the lawn which once surrounded the building is cut by a road running to a housing estate. There is a red granite cross at the east end, its plinth half covered with the pale stems of grass. The Church of England does not want to use the chapel any more, the Roman Catholics and the Non-conformists have surveyed it but do not find it convenient.

One of the first English clock-towers was built at Westminster in 1288. A Judge called Ralph de Higham was fined for tampering with a Court Roll, and the money was spent on building the tower and providing one bell, Great Tom of Westminster. Later a clock struck the hours and reminded the judges in Westminster Hall of the motto on its face, "Discite Justitiam Monite et non temnere divis". Great Tom was taken down and sold to St. Paul's Cathedral, which used the metal to cast the hour bell which chimes when the monarch dies. It replaced the bell John Hatfield heard strike thirteen times at midnight while on sentry duty on the terrace of Windsor Castle. He was court-martialled for being asleep at his post, for no one believed his story until people came and said that it was true. He died, aged one hundred and two, in 1722.

For the present Palace of Westminster, Sir Charles Barry and Pugin designed the clock-tower to take a clock and bells worthy of a dignified building and institution. The tower is three hundred feet high, and both it and the Victoria Tower are as bulky as the blocks of flats which architects would like to build today, but which they are prevented from doing by laws restricting the height of buildings. Anyone who objects to tall buildings should walk round the Kingsbury district of Hendon, and then walk from Harrow to Sudbury Hill and look towards Windsor and see the little houses spread below him, the unnecessary roads connecting them up, and the beautiful contour of the land which can still just be seen lying beneath them.

The present clock and bells at Westminster were designed by Edmund Beckett Denison, who later became Lord Grimthorpe. He made a fortune at the Bar, was an amateur architect, one of the first people to work out mathematically the relationship between the shape and weight of a bell and its musical note, and President of the Horological Institute for thirty-seven years. He wrote a book called *A Rudimentary Treatise on Clocks, Watches and Bells*, which went through many editions; the title is one of his few pieces of modesty, for he was one of the rudest and most crotchety of men. In the last part of his life he spent a quarter of a million pounds on the restoration of St. Albans Abbey.

The hour bell at Westminster was cast by Warner's in 1856 at Norton, near Stockton-on-Tees. The metal was melted twice and then run into a reservoir, and from there to the mould which was sunk into the floor and tamped round with sand. The bell weighed sixteen tons and had the inscription, "Cast in the twentieth year of the reign of her Majesty Queen Victoria, and in the year of our Lord 1856, from the design of Edmund Beckett Denison, Q.C.; Sir Benjamin Hall Bart, Chief Commissioner of Works". Warner's trade-mark of the Royal arms was stamped on the waist with "John Warner and Sons, Crescent Foundry, Cripplegate, London". It went from Norton to West Hartlepool by rail, and from there to Maudsley's Wharf in London on board the *Wave*. Finally sixteen horses dragged it through the street to the foot of the Clock Tower at Westminster.

By now the bell had been nicknamed Big Ben after Sir Benjamin Hall, but one of the things the designer did not really know was how heavy the hammer should be to bring out the fullest note. So he hung the bell from a cat gallows at the foot of the tower, and started to experiment with increasingly heavy hammers till he cracked it. The

153

Illustrated London News was very much opposed to Lord Grimthorpe at this time, and thought this an immense joke and when, over a year later, on Thursday, February 18th, 1858, the first Big Ben was broken up by having a twenty-four hundredweight iron ball dropped on to it, said: "The Savants, Rev. Taylor and E. B. Denison came as mourners of the bell about which the latter had discoursed so minutely to the great delight of the members of the Royal Institution." The pieces were taken to Mears' foundry at Whitechapel.

The template for the Big Ben which we hear today is now an arch round the front door of Mears and Stainbanks' office at Whitechapel, and the gauge for the bell hangs in the foundry. Big Ben is inscribed: "This bell was cast by George Mears of Whitechapel for the clock of the House of Parliament, under the direction of Edmund Beckett Denison Q.C. in the 21st year of the reign of Queen Victoria, in the year of our Lord MDCCCLVIII." Again sixteen horses dressed with flowers and ribbons, their drivers walking beside them, drew the bell through the Borough to Westminster. At the foot of the tower it was laid on its side on a cradle which was pushed into the shaft running up the tower. This shaft was lined with wood, and the bell was pulled up it to the top by a special chain one thousand six hundred feet long made by Messrs. Crawshaw of Newcastle. Big Ben is nine feet in diameter, seven feet six inches high, and weighs thirteen tons, ten hundredweight, three quarters, and fifteen pounds.

When Mears accepted the contract to make the bell, he stipulated that it was not to be struck with a hammer heavier than four hundredweight. The clock struck perfectly for two months, and then it was discovered that the bell was cracked. Lord Grimthorpe said that this was not caused by the hammer, but had been there since the bell was cast and that Mears had concealed it with cement and paint; but it was found that the hammer weighed seven hundredweight and not four. For three years the hours were struck on the fourth quarter bell, and then Big Ben was turned round slightly and a four hundredweight clapper fitted. Though cracked it has rung ever since.

Lord Grimthorpe spent his money on St. Albans Abbey; the Baroness Burdett-Coutts spent hers on humanity, in particular on the people living in the slums in Westminster and Bethnal Green. She knew that religion and education, as well as a stomach full of palatable food, made people's lives happier, and in building schools, churches, and markets she became one of the great patrons of bell-founding.

She was the youngest of six children of Sir Francis Burdett, the Whig Member of Parliament for Westminster, and her mother was the youngest daughter, by his first wife, of Thomas Coutts, of Coutts' Bank.

In 1815, Thomas Coutts married as his second wife Harriet Mellon the actress, who had played such parts as Sherry in the *Beaux Stratagem* and Miss Prue in *Love for Love*. She had a following in the theatres in which she appeared, possessed a good figure, and was a jolly and sensible woman. She had been Coutts' mistress for some time, and when he died in 1822 he left her his fortune of £900,000 and a share in the bank. On June 16th, 1827, Harriet Coutts married the 9th Duke of St. Albans.

In 1837 Harriet Mellon died and left her fortune to Angela Burdett. In the autumn of that year Angela Burdett-Coutts, as she was now called, moved into her step-grandmother's house at 1 Stratton Street, and began the philanthropic work which occupied the rest of her life. Queen Victoria was one of her greatest admirers, and sent her a piece of Herne's Oak from Windsor forest to make a casket for her first-folio Shakespeare.

The first church which she built—as a memorial to her father—was St. Stephen's, Rochester Row, in Westminster. But the church, she considered, must be supported by schools, Bible classes, and soup kitchens, and in Westminster she provided an education for children of all ages; she was the first person to start sewing and cooking classes

155

in schools and she founded the Westminster Technical
Institute in 1893. She built three more churches in London
and another St. Stephen's in Carlisle, and in 1877 she gave
four of the new ring of twelve bells to St. Paul's

In 1860, as a result of a treaty with France, it became
possible to import into this country silk which could be
sold at a lower price than that made by the weavers of
Shoreditch and Bethnal Green, and thousands of weavers
found they had no means of supporting their families. The
Baroness Burdett-Coutts enabled many of these to emigrate
to Canada and Australia, and her work in these two districts of London spread to all the poor there. Some of her
organisations sound quaint, but the Destitute Children's
Dinner Society, of which she was President, is no longer
needed because as an ultimate result of its work every
child can get a meal at school. She helped to start the Shoe-
blacks' Brigade and the Flower Girls' Brigade, which are
extinct because of the changes in the condition of life which
she and others like her brought about. She encouraged
gloss and blackened hoofs for costers' donkeys by building model donkey stables; for which the costermongers
presented her with a silver donkey in 1875, and she started
a movement for making poor cottagers keep goats.

One of the most morally depressing and architecturally
derelict districts of Bethnal Green in the middle of the last
century was Nova Scotia Gardens, which was situated between the present-day Columbia Road and Hackney Road.
In 1862 the Baroness built four model tenements here
called Columbia Square, and the design was so impressive
that they were used as a basis for all the Peabody Buildings.

In 1865 she built Holly Village at the bottom of Highgate
Hill on part of the garden of her house, Holly Lodge, so
that poor people could live in the country. The entrance
is through a gateway between two of the houses, and immediately inside are two more, each with a tower, half-
timbered and miniature, their tops crowned with a multi-
plicity of crocketed and finialed turrets in wood and metal-

work. Beyond these the village green widens out, and the remainder of the houses are grouped round a rectangle of terraced lawns. If the inhabitants were to live the country life, then they must have real country houses, and each one is a miniature of the merchants' palaces built at this time on the outskirts of Bristol and Manchester behind barricades of fir trees and laurels. Inside, the light pours into the rooms through the Gothic windows, the tiny grates are surrounded by tiles, painted with groups of shells in borders of black and sienna. One of the kitchen ranges, small, knobby, and ingeniously designed, is called the "Bell Portable"—and that must be sufficient excuse for this digression. The whole village is clearly the conception of a woman who saw philanthropy not so much as a worthy moral act for the improvement of people but as a means of encouraging them to find increased pleasure and enjoyment in their lives and surroundings.

But to return to Bethnal Green; in 1864 Baroness Burdett-Coutts started the Columbia Market project, and in 1866 a Private Act of Parliament was passed to enable her to build it. The object was to allow the poor to buy their food as fresh and as cheap as possible; costers would be able to hire their carts and barrows from the market for nearly nothing, and they would be able to buy stock without giving a profit to an unnecessary middleman. The people who lived in Columbia Square would be able to buy food from the market, and the building itself was to include houses for city clerks who found that they had to travel a long way into the suburbs to find houses suitable to their status; each house in the market was to have a separate front door so that they should not feel that they were living in a tenement. She had, however, under-estimated the strength of the suppliers of food to London, who combined against the market when it opened in 1869; they were so successful that it soon had to close. It was reopened as a wholesale fish market, and failed. She transferred it to the Corporation of London in 1871, but it came back to her in 1874. In 1875 she arranged with three railway companies to secure supplies of fish, but Billingsgate successfully sabotaged this attempt and she had to stop. In 1884 she obtained a new Act of Parliament to operate the market with a special fleet of fishing-boats and special arrangements with the railways, but again the opposition was too strong. The market was a failure, but she did draw attention to the inefficient way food was distributed in London, with the result that five markets, including Billingsgate, were rebuilt in the fifteen years after the Columbia Market opened, and although she did not succeed in her particular object, the Baroness achieved this more general one, at a cost of a quarter of a million pounds, the price of the Columbia Market.

The architect was Henry Ashley Darbishire, who designed it in the form of a quadrangle with the main hall as the block opposite the entrance, the clerk's houses with shops beneath them joined the other three sides. The ground of the quadrangle was of black granite divided into squares with lines of red granite, and each of these was a trader's pitch. The main hall was one hundred feet long, fifty feet wide, and fifty feet high, the interior was divided into seven bays by granite pillars, and behind these set in the bays were twenty-four small shops, thirteen feet deep, six feet wide, and eight feet high, with an office, a fireplace, running water, and a sink; the walls of these were of polished Irish granite so that they could be washed down easily. Above the shops was a gallery where flowers, fruit, and root vegetables could be sold, and the central space of the hall was for general trade. There was a coffee-shop and a tavern for refreshments in one corner of the quadrangle; life must be fun and enjoyable, even at the risk of some people getting drunk.

Angela Burdett-Coutts felt that a beautiful building which the people could use every day would improve them more than a museum, and her ideas are mirrored in the article which *The Builder* printed about the market.

"Place objects of beauty among the people, and you create by their means in process of time that very taste and perception which are needed to appreciate them. . . . Nothing can be truer than the assertion that human beings inevitably become assimilated to their material surroundings. One would no more expect to gather 'grapes of thorns and figs of thistles' than to find either refinement of mind or manner, or grace of life or person, in such a district as Bethnal Green. The work which owes its existence to the large-hearted yet prudent charity of Baroness Burdett-Coutts is exactly of that kind to afford real pleasure from the conviction that it must raise the whole tone of life and taste in the people who surround it; and who in their daily life and avocations can no more escape from the beneficial influence which such work exerts, than they can avoid, in the contrary case, the degradation which is produced among large masses of population by filth, and squalor, and the usual accompaniments of great poverty."

When the market opened at the end of April 1869, many people thought far too much money had been spent and that the design was too elaborate, forgetting that the richly carved stone and wood decorations were to give work to the out-of-work masons and carvers of Bethnal Green. The whole building is in "the second pointed style". There are mottoes round the door which we can find comic, for· getting what this part of London was like at the time, crockets and finials sprout from the roof, and there is a charming little water-tower. But the climax of the composition is the hall. Any Flemish guild would have been proud to possess this in the late Middle Ages, for it is encrusted with ornaments. The roof is supported on slender columns of polished granite, and the vaulting itself is of the best pitch pine. A tower one hundred and fifteen feet high rises above the entrance, and at the top there is a clock with chimes and eight jacks.

The L.C.C. today uses the market as a store for building materials, piles of reinforcing rod lie in the quadrangle, and the hall is filled with lavatory pans, die-cast lead work, screws and in this medieval hall the proper medieval fixings

159

which we still use in our building. The polished marble shops are obscured, and everything is dusty and unloved.

To climb the tower to the clock one goes up a ladder which rises almost vertically in the hollow body of the tower. Pigeons fly around one, and the rungs are dirty with rust and their droppings. At the top of the ladder is a platform, and in one corner, low down between two pigeons' nests, a little door opens on to a platform at the back of the tower. Another ladder rises vertically against the outside wall to another platform level with the jacks, and one more ladder goes up again to the clock, which is now no longer used.

The clock jacks stand two to each side of the tower and face in towards their partners; they are about nine feet tall, and are carved of wood to represent medieval Flemish artisans. One arm of each is bent at the elbow, and in that hand is a metal hammer with which he strikes the bell in front of him. The dirt and dust of London lies between their necks and shirts, powders their beards, and rests in the convolutions of their ears. It is not a gay octet, they were carved to represent the ideal worker who, given time and encouragement, might in a few years buy food in the market below. Their faces are nobly sorrowful, earnest, intent on craft, at home they have large, beautiful wives and straight-limbed sons. They are stable and secure, perfectly content with their station in life.

The clock jacks of the Middle Ages were also individuals. One of the armed men who strike the bell at Wells Cathedral has a noble, firm face; the other is weaker and demure. They are in no sense caricatures, and the only parts of them which are not as elegant and refined as possible are their moving arms, thickened and deformed for strength. The horsemen who charge round and fight each other at the hour inside the cathedral are caricatures of knights, and the one who wins beats the other with a caddish sideways sweep of his lance. There are a number of other clock jacks in this country, their quality naturally

160

varying with the skill of the men who made them. The armed men are elegant and the knights are caricatures deliberately; Jack Blandifer, the third jack in Wells, is carved and painted in the same convention as the figures on a roundabout organ to alarm and mystify the simple minded. The two seventeenth-century cherubs at Rye, who stand on either side of the inscription "For our time is a very shadow that passeth away" and strike the bell, are bad but comic pieces of carving; and most of the other jacks in this country are variations of quaintness. The eight men at the Columbia Market, the two armed men outside Wells Cathedral, and the two little knights inside are the only examples which can be considered works of art, good or bad as you prefer. Two jacks that are interesting because of their history are Gog and Magog on St. Dunstan's Church in Fleet Street. They were made in 1671, and the space in front of the church became a great site for pickpockets, who would work on country bumpkins who came to see the clock. In 1830, the clock was bought by the Marquess of Hertford, and put in a special tower at his house, St. Dunstan's Villa in Regents Park. This was demolished just before the last war, and a neo-Georgian one built in its place. The clock jacks went back to St. Dunstan's Church.

Columbia Market had a special set of bells for the chimes to be played upon, but when church bells are used for chimes, the number, which is seldom more than twelve, limits the number of tunes which can be played, so that many churches and tower clocks which chime at the hours play the same tune and some churches combine secular songs with hymn-tunes in their chimes. "Lady Chatham's Jigg", "Lovely Nancy", "Rousseau's Dream", and "Life Let Us Cherish" being mixed with religious pieces.

A refinement of chimes is the carillon, which has the great advantage that it can range from two octaves on twenty-three bells to five-and-a-half octaves on seventy-two bells, and naturally there will be a much wider choice of music for it to play. The Americans, the Dutch, and the Belgians are more attracted by them than we are, and the carillon at the Riverside Church in New York has seventy-two bells, the heaviest weighing eighteen tons, five hundred-weight. The bells are rung by striking the keys of a clavier, and the carilloneur or bell organist can strike loud or soft to alter the volume. The main criticism of carillon playing which can be made is that the melody is too often vitiated by florid playing, by unnecessary grace notes and arpeggios. The carillon can be played by a machine, though then the volume cannot be altered. In England carillons can be heard at Eaton Hall, Bournville, Loughborough, Parkgate, and at Atkinson's in Bond Street. This country is more renowned for their manufacture than for their use.

Bells which were infrequently made in this country but which were heard in every middle class home in the last century were the bells standing in a row by the cylinder in a musical box. They usually have patterns engraved on them and are almost the only bells outside a church tower which bear any decoration at all. In the orchestra, the Glockenspiel and Celesta, though these are not bells but flat steel plates, tinkle away for sugar plum fairies, or sleigh bells jingling through the snow. An instrument we no longer hear is the Cherubine Minor invented by Henry Whittaker. One single keyboard controlled a harp, an organ, and glass bells. Glass is a more resonant imitation of bell metal than china or plastic, and the glass bells made by bored glass blowers as individual *tours de force* are even prettier than the paper ones we hang up at Christmas.

Silent like paper or sounding like glass, at will, are the bells in the Campana Mutaphone, a machine made and invented by Henry Carter. It is now in the Science Museum, and can ring changes in any method on any number of bells up to twelve automatically, draw the skeleton course of a bell on a roll of paper, and if desired draw the course without ringing. The technical zenith of change ringing has here become silence.

162

9

Drowned Bells and Bells Brands

DABBLERS see the paraphernalia of art as a badge to set them apart from the philistines, and may extol the medium above the object they have made, making travail more important than the child. Professional painters do not hang palettes set with a complete range of colours on their drawing-room walls as trophies, nor do engine-drivers make topiary reproductions of the Flying Scot in the front gardens of their homes, they have enough of engines during their work. The railway maniac, though, constructs a microcosm of Willesden Junction in his back bedroom, knows Bradshaw by heart, and can decipher the monograms of companies before amalgamation; and the amateur water-colour painter, finding such a picturesque subject as a Cotswold manor-house set in a froth of herbaceous borders, needs the most complex and expensive equipment to do the old stone and woolly delphiniums justice. Polished mahogany boxes for paints, a choice of over one hundred and fifty colours.

japanned boxes for brushes, collapsible water-pots, dark green camp-stools, umbrellas, shady hats, can all be bought, as well as paper like a mandarin's quilted coat to paint on; and, for use in the home, the messier oil paints, ordered rows of two hundred colours in shining tubes carefully rolled from the bottom. I am sure that in the stables of some house there lies a lady's sketching cart; the body would be lightly built of wicker, with exquisite drawers of dark wood shaped inside, like a dressing-case to take the pots and brushes. In this cart she could wander round the park taking portraits of the landscape, having trouble with the foreshortening of sheep and cows. Mr. Birkett Foster in another field would be using only a few paints in a dirty old chocolate tin.

So for the bell-ringers. They know bells too well to bother about their representation or to have miniatures of them or extraordinary pieces of nonsense like special ringing gloves.

But, before their lives were straitened by reforming clergymen, the ringers had one piece of fancy equipment, great jugs or gotches, in which to carry their evening's beer to the belfry. Perhaps it was used for milk or water by one of them on other days, or perhaps it was a special one in pink or blue china, kept in the belfry, or one given to them by a friend, inscribed with the ineluctable doggerel, and holding four gallons of beer. At Norwich there is one dated 1676 and inscribed:

> Come brother shall we join?
> Give me your twopence, here is mine.

The Welsh are more noted for their bell-like voices than for their ringing, but at Swansea a jug bore this poem scratched beneath the glaze.

> Come fill me full with liquor sweet,
> For that is good when friends do meet;
> When I am full then drink about:
> I ne'er will fail till all is out.

In East Anglia, though drink and jollity were not allowed to disrupt the singles and tittums, the Beccles ringers had this verse on their jug:

> *When I am filled with liquor strong*
> *Each man drink once and then ding dong.*
> *Drink not too much to cloud your knobbs.*
> *Lest you forget to make the bobbs.*

Bells and bell ringing, unlike railway trains and water-colour painting, are unable to offer the attraction of numberless gadgets, and are no fun for the amateur; a devotee or nothing is the only rule. But the bell, like the sleigh and the Muscovy winter, has a firm niche in that file of the collective unconscious labelled "Folk-lore and Legend", as well as appearing fairly frequently in the *Trade-marks Journal*.

Bell, the mind thinks, and bumbles off through the undergrowth; bell may become belle, evoking first an image of Pullman Cars and then of Southern Belles, those julep-drinking girls in one's private vision of life south of the mysterious Mason Dixon Line, whose brothers or lovers are ready to avenge at once and with pistols, any injury done to their honour.

Belles-lettres too; spurned now by those academics who select a first eleven to represent English Literature, which has Eliot, T. S., as centre forward, and Eliot, George, in goal; Pater, W., is not even in the "C" team. But if the æsthetes do not rate an England Cap, dignified prose of a fine curly kind is represented by John Donne, transferred from the *Memento Mori* eleven.

Donne is the prose writer who has done most for bells as figures in art. His *Devotions Upon Emergent Occasions*, a series of twenty-three Meditations, Expostulations, and Prayers on his illness, has in it the great bell phrase. Donne was a victim of accidie; before he was ordained he: "Spent all my time in consulting how I should spend it", and this complaint leaves scar tissue, unlike Tinnitus Aurium—the continual chirping, hissing, rustling of leaves, boiling of kettles, rushing of water, rumbling of carts, ringing of bells, escape of gas, blowing off steam, "Telegraph Wires", æolian harp, clicking, pumping, musical notes, voices talking and voices singing, which are symptoms of aural disease and disappear with their cause; accidie diverts thought towards bones and the grave, to the centre of "nature's nest of boxes"; death becomes the centre of man, and the passing bell, the warning of death.

The heading of Donne's sixteenth section is, "From the Bells of the church adjoyning, I am daily remembered of my buriall in the funeralls of others". The seventeenth heading is "Now this bell tolling softly for another, saies to me, thou must die", and the eighteenth "The bell rings out and tells me in him that I am dead". In each of them he uses the bells as a start for meditating on death, and Christ the victor of death. The seventeenth meditation has in it the sentence "No man is an *Iland*, intire of it selfe; every man is a peece of the *Continent*, a part of the *maine*; if a *Clod* bee washed away by the *Sea, Europe* is the lesse, as well as if a *Promontorie* were, as well as if a *Mannor* of thy *friends* or of *thine owne* were; any mans *death* diminishes *me*, because I am involved in *Mankinde*; And therefore never send to know for whom the *bell* tolls; It tolls for *thee*." There in the midde of the page is Ernest Hemingway tolling *his* bell.

If Donne is the high spot of Bell prose writers, who is to represent poetry? There are forty-four lines with the word bell in the Shakespeare concordance; Tennyson has a column and a half in his; there are Poe and Jean Ingelow, and Moore, but bells unfortunately bring out the worst in poets, and we may prefer a good low poet to a good poet in an off moment; such a poet as Arthur Cleveland Coxe, at one time Bishop of Western New York, some of whose Christian ballads were published in 1849. First, two lines to give his background:

> . . . *Bless the Lord that I am sprung*
> *Of good old English line.*

166

Now two verses from his ballad on bells:

Those bells and chimes of Motherland
Upon a Christmas morn.
Out breaking, as the angels did,
For a redeemer born.
How merrily they call afar
To cot and Baron's hall,
With holly deck'd and mistletoe
To keep the Festival.

The chimes of England how they peal
From tower and Gothic pile,
Where hymn and swelling anthem fill
The dim cathedral aisle,
Where windows bathe the holy light
On priestly heads that falls,
And stain the florid tracery
And banner-dighted walls.

But no known poet can compete with the anonymous
bell poetry of the nursery and the street. From the cradle
Ding Dong Bell means poor pussy in the well and not
"What a world of solemn thought their monody com-
pels". At parties one used to play oranges and lemons while
this rhyme was chanted.

Oranges and Lemons
Say the Bells of St. Clement's.
You owe me five farthings,
Say the Bells of St. Martin's.
When will you pay me?
Say the Bells of Old Bailey.
When I grow rich
Say the Bells of Shoreditch.
When will that be?
Say the Bells of Stepney.
I'm sure I don't know
Says the great Bell at Bow.
Here comes a candle to light you to bed
Here comes a chopper to chop off your head.

167

St. Clement's Eastcheap and St. Clement Danes, both claim to say Oranges and Lemons; there is an excellent short history of their quarrel in Iona and Peter Opie's *Dictionary of Nursery Rhymes*. St. Clement Danes is perhaps winning; a service was held there every March, when members of the Danish Community presented oranges and lemons to all children who came to church on that day.

Children get all the best bell poetry. When they were running races pretending to be horses, centaurs smacking their own flanks to drive themselves to a greater pace, the race would be started with this rhyme:

> *Bell horses, Bell horses*
> *What time of day,*
> *One o'clock, two o'clock,*
> *Off and away.*

At the last line they would run off.

For adults there is the verse in the ballad "Lucey and Colin" about the bell and raven (based on the belief that the ringing of bells by poltergeists or as Tinnitus Aurium in the head was a sign that someone was soon to die) and it is much more compelling than any of Jean Ingelow's artful rhymes:

> *Three times all in the dead of night*
> *A bell was heard to ring,*
> *And at her window shrieking thrice*
> *The raven flapp'd his wing.*

Some bells are supposed to sing a verse; if you listen to call-change ringers who ring in the same order for a time, the bells will soon start to make a jumble of words, which one forgets directly they make the next change. But some villages have preserved the words their bells made. Hittisleigh's in Devon said:

> *My Dog Bite thy Dog's tail,*
> *Thy Dog Bite my Dog's tail.*

168

At Kettering the chimes said:

> *Joe Timms, Joe Timms,*
> *Come lend me your limbs,*
> *And I'll lend you mine tomorrow.*
> *I love my life*
> *As I love my wife*
> *But I'll neither lend nor borrow.*

At Ware they retold a variation of the fairly common custom of selling a wife. (No bells commemorate the less common husband sale at Totnes when a wife sold her husband for two shillings to an old woman, refusing a bid of one and sixpence from a girl.)

> *Lend me your wife today,*
> *I'll lend you mine tomorrow.*
> *No, I'll be like the chimes of Ware,*
> *I'll neither lend nor borrow.*

One rhyme for children has bells in a less pleasant context. In *Flowers of Instruction or Familiar Subjects in Verse,* by Mary Elliott, published in 1820, a poem called the "Lost Child" has a whole page illustration of this verse.

> *The Showman with Grotto of shells,*
> *Induc'd little Lucy to go*
> *She has followed his musical bells*
> *And her mother forgot for the show.*

Lucy is gazing through the windows of the doll's-house-like grotto, seeing the dimly reflecting spar, or perhaps a room of the kind created by M. R. James. Behind her stands the showman; in his cap are two bells, and in each hand three more which he rings above his head; in a few minutes the sun will set, and he will commit another horrid crime, leaving only her crumpled sash as a clue for the faithful bloodhounds.

The showman enticing little children to him with his bells is no nastier than a game which could be played with a cat and a bell in the seventeenth century. John White—

he called himself a lover of artificial conclusions—published during the Civil War a jest book called *A Rich Cabinet with Variety of Inventions*. It is one of the earliest books for those who are socially unsure of themselves, and who feel that if they can make people laugh they will be instantly loved. John White tells them how to make fireworks useful both in peace and war, how to refresh old pictures to make them look as if they were new, or such tricks as how to hang a pail of water upon a stick and nothing to support it. One of his ideas is to have dainty sport with a cat. You take your hostess' favourite tib and your host's favourite hawk bell and a piece of strong thin string from your dirty doublet, and tie the bell tightly to the cat's tail, the pain of the tight string will make it lash, and the ringing of the bell will frighten it, then you sit back and laugh while poor pussy scuttles round the room. If you had had walnuts for dinner and there was some hot pitch handy, you filled half shells with pitch and stuck them to the cat's feet and watched it try to run away.

Other games used bells, particularly at Shrove Tuesday, when, says Taylor the Water Poet:

> "Here must enter that wadling, stradling, bursten-gutted Carnifex of all Christendoms, vulgarly enstiled Shrove Tuesday, but more pertinently, Sole Monarch of the Mouth, High Steward of the Stomack, Chiefe Ganimede to the Guts, Prime Peer of the Pullets, First Favourite to the Frying Pans, Greatest Basawon to the Batter Bowles, Protector of the Pancakes, First Founder of the Fritters, Baron of the Bacon Flitch, Earle of the Egg Baskets."

Shrove Tuesday was a day of sports of varying kinds; at Norwich in 1440 John Gladman organised a pageant of the seasons of the year. Lent wore a coat of white and red herrings' skins and his horse had clothing of oyster shells, being also "Trappyd with tynnfoyle and other nyse disgisy things". But this was sissy stuff, for in other parts of England they were burning holly boys and ivy girls, and Threshing the Fat Hen:

"The Hen was hung at a fellow's back, who had also some horse bells about him, the rest of the fellows were blinded and had boughs in their hands, with which they chased this fellow, and his hen about some large court or small enclosure. The fellow with this hen and bells shifting as well as he could, they followed the sound, and sometimes struck him and his hen; other times, if he could yet get behind one of them, they threshed one another, but the jest was, the maids were to blind the fellows, which they did with their apron, and indulged their sweethearts with a peeping-hole, which the other looked out as sharp to prevent. After this the hen was boiled with bacon, and stores of pancakes and fritters were provided. Lazy or sluttish maids were presented with the first pancakes, which they would not own. In Wales hens who did not lay eggs before Shrove Tuesday were threshed by a man with a flail; if he struck and killed them he had them for his pains.":

Brand's *Popular Antiquities.*

Sadists cannot get much pleasure out of horse-racing, the horses are so morbidly sensitive that they have to be wrapped in the best woollen blankets and fed hot possets to soothe their nerves before they run in a race. Racing though is connected with bells which were used for prizes before the introduction of selling plates and rose bowls. The first race for a bell was run on the Roodee at Chester in 1539, and from that date until 1624, when the race was reorganised by John Brereton, the bell was competed for each year. Brereton increased the length of the course to five times round the Roodee, and allowed the winner to keep the bell. Later, at the beginning of the eighteenth century, bells were abandoned and money prizes were raced for, purses of so many guineas, or, at the smaller meetings, a bridle, or a saddle, or a set of horse trappings. From this use of a bell as a prize comes the phrase "To bear away the bell".

An epitaph in Camden's *Remains* is as follows:

Here lyes the man whose horse did gain
The bell, in race on Salisbury Plain.

171

"To bear away the bell" must not be confused with "To bear the bell". The first of these means to win the prize and the second to be first, or in the front rank, or the cow or sheep which carries the bell and leads the flock or herd; as Jean Ingelow says:

> Come uppe Jetty, follow, follow,
> Jetty to the milking shed.

But though one can bear the bell and still be respected, to be a bell-wether is to be a fool, and instead of "to lose the bell", meaning that you have cast off your stupidity or wetherdom, it means that one was unfortunate to lose a race, similarly "to deserve a bell" is no sign of folly but the equivalent of being a favourite for a race.

More of these nutty phrases and proverbs use bells as their image, but they are seldom heard now. "He is like a bell that will go for anyone that pulls it"; "He who cannot bear the clapper should not pull the bell"; "As the bell clinks so the fool thinks"; "Fear not the loss of the bells more than the loss of the steeple". All these are like the colloquial phrases in an old French grammar, collections of words and thoughts which are never uttered or put together by anyone. "Give her the Bells and let her fly", which can be interpreted as "Don't throw good money after bad", is the equivalent of "That butler is skilled but my uncle's is humbler"; both should be in the ideas museum. There are three phrases which are still common; "As clear as a bell", "As sound as a bell", and "Drowned bell". The first two need no explanation, the third is perhaps more obscure and is used in the arts to refer to the use of an echo from someone else's work. The poets of this century have perfected this technique, and for a convenient collection of examples there can be nothing better than *The Waste Land,* by T. S. Eliot. There are, though, many stories of real drowned and subterranean bells; and drowning men and women hear bells ringing as they sink beneath the waves. At Tunstall in Norfolk is a pond called

Hell Hole; in the summer bubbles rise to the surface of
the water from the sinking bells of a nearby church, which
were stolen by the devil and cast into it.

The drowned bells of Aberdovey in Wales are first mentioned in Dibden's *Liberty Hall*.

> *Os wit I yng carrie i,*
> *Rwi fy dwyn dy garrie di*
> *As ein dai tre pewdar pimp chwek,*
> *Go the bells of Aberdovey.*

There is also the story that the giant Idris dropped his
bell into the estuary, which is heard at certain states of the
tide.

Near Kirby Lonsdale there is a hollow in the ground
where a church, and congregation, were swallowed up and
the bells can be heard ringing on Sundays; as they can at
Blackpool, where a church was submerged by the sea. At
Raleigh in Nottinghamshire there is a tradition of a village
obliterated by an earthquake, and bells can be heard ringing in the ground on Christmas morning. Two more
proverbs must be mentioned. "To bell the cat", from the
fable of the mice who wished to do this, which means to
undertake a perilous part, or be the ringleader in any
undertaking, and "Hang all one's bells on one horse",
meaning to leave all one's money to one child.

Horses and bells seem to combine well together, there
are proverbs, and rhymes, and terret bells ringing remain
so clearly from the impression of a well-dressed horse that
a Bell-horse is a horse with its mane and tail plaited with
ribbons and straw, decked with flowers for a May Day
Parade.

There is also Bell-bastard, the child of a woman who
is herself illegitimate, and Bell-comb, the accumulated
grease from the gudgeons, considered efficacious as a
remedy for rheumatism, ringworm, and shingles. If you
get shingles, you will die if the swollen red patches meet
in a circle round your body; to prevent this rub in some

173

Bell-comb. A Bell-rope is another word for a fore-lock, and Bell-moth is a moth.

The most common use of bell in compound nouns is to describe something shaped like a bell—bell-bottomed trousers—and particularly flowers, which with one exception are all of a nasty kind. Blue-bells need no further comment; bell-rose is a Somerset dialect name for the daffodil; the bell-glass is a forcing glass to be placed over tender plants; and the bell-binder, the best of these bell flowers, is the large wild convolvulus. Canterbury Bells were originally the bells worn by pilgrims to Canterbury, and as a flower name referred to the Throat Wort or Nettle-leaved Bell Flower, Campanula trachelium; then the name was transferred to the cultivated exotic Campanula medium, called in the sixteenth century Coventry Bells or Marian's Violet. These are the woolliest flowers. They represent the decline and fall of the English picturesque movement, when the landscape, instead of being made to compose round a group of figures, a crisp building, or a rugged piece of natural rock, sprawls and meanders, loose and weak. Avenues of cypress lead to no artifact or vista, but to a dumpy stone seat. A feature started instantly dies in a mess of crazy-paving on the lawn, musical comedy roses foam round doorways, and at the slightest glimmer of sun one is made to eat out of doors, with the wind cooling the dishes and turning napkins and clothes into sails; this is the best setting for Campanula medium and Campanula calycanthema, which can be bought in a good range of blues, whites, and mauves, and in a fondant or tart's-knicker pink.

The word bell has other connotations; as a noun it describes the fruition of hops, which are said to be in bell; and as a verb, to bell, it means to bubble, or the noise of stags in the rutting season; but the bell as the everted orifice of a wind instrument has the most interesting application, evoking a world as distinct as the ringers', and one to which a digression must be made.

Brass bandsmen can best be observed at a brass band contest. Pom-pomming away beneath the curly canopies of cast-iron which protect them from the sun and rain, at the seaside or embedded in the pink roses and lawns of a municipal park, they are too serenely smug, they are above the world and have no rivals, their bodies supported by the gold embroidery on their tunics, and their minds swirling to the strains of some "Pot Pourri", old English tunes, sea shanties, waltzes, mazurkas, marches, and two-steps. But at a contest, when the streets and gardens of a town are filled with bandsmen, they have rivals for musical skill and for magnificent uniforms, and they lose the grandeur of elevated isolation.

The contest will start in the morning with each band marching down the street, past the judges who are in a sealed room like the judges at a ringing competition; in the afternoon they play their test piece in the bandstand. This music is designed to exploit every instrument in the band, at every pace and pitch, piano passages will be sustained on the windy blowings of euphoniums, while the cornets imitate violins; the basic principle of brass band music being that if they can stir the stomach so easily with marches and dances, they must also try to move the soul with transcriptions of symphonies.

Fortunately the brass band movement is beginning to revive again after the interruption of the war, and at Fairford in Gloucestershire, where the annual carnival was held again in 1953 for the first time since 1939, the bands played throughout the afternoon in a ring in the park far away from the large arena where tractors raced up and down, and the floats of the pageant—the bicycles disguised with paper and the decorated perambulators—were judged. The bandstand was a temporary one of tubular scaffolding wound round with dark red and yellow bunting, and here, sitting on yellow chairs, they played "Golden Dawn". Some of the bands were in uniforms, which with the increase in cost are not so fine as they were before the war, so that the men look less like officers in a crack Austrian regiment, and more like the men who control the queues outside cinemas. Some bands were in mufti, and many had lady cornettists, both uniformed and un-uniformed. If you are not very interested in music the conductor is the man to watch. Some have a high-class technique derived from the conductors of symphony orchestras, large flowing gestures, sculpting the music in the air around them. But the most usual style is very properly derived from the masters of military bands, whose aim is an absolute economy of movement, one bossy, white-gloved little finger moving through an inch making a change from the quietest gusty hush to the full roar of the tornado; but this method has the disadvantage that the conductor may constrain his urge to wave his baton wildly in the air with such energy that he seems to be enduring the attack of a terrible muscular spasm, which racks his whole body, face, and arms with the most minute but violent twitching. The day always ends with a massed-band concert, and before this the bandsmen can be seen walking about the town and gardens, drinking cups of tea or admiring the instruments laid out on the stands of manufacturers and music-shop keepers, who make arrangements of sousaphones and trombones on black velvet, their bells polished and engraved with name and trademark.

Bandsmen use for their badge the lyre, which as a symbol is limited in its uses to the musical arts or truly refined commercial products. The bell, though, a more robust and vulgar instrument, has been widely used as an emblem. In heraldry it is almost invariably a rebus; a man called Bell might have one on his arms or for his crest, and a branch of the Dobell family has for arms, sable a hind passant between three bells argent. Heraldry, unfortunately, calls crotals, hawk's bells, so that if one were fortunate enough to bear a belled cat for a crest it could never be crotally gorged.

The publican was one of the first people to use the bell as a sign. There is no central register of inn signs, so it is impossible to say how many Bell Inns there are in England, but Larwood and Hotten say that it is one of the commonest names. Besides plain Bell, they recorded such everyday variants as the Six Bells, the Ring of Bells, The Ringers, and some charming and obscure compound names, The Bell and Cuckoo, The Bell and Bullock, The Bell and Mackerel, and The Bell and Neats Tongue, which are the result of the publican paying a compliment to the ringers, who would be some of his best customers, by adding the bell to the existing sign.

In the eighteenth century a publican who kept a Bell Inn would print his trade card with his name and address, and a reminder that he could supply "Neat Post Chaises" or "Post Chaises with Able Horses", and a small picture of a bell. Eighteenth-century advertising was restricted by the idea that the Nobility, Gentry, and Clergy were the only markets to whom an appeal should be directed, and consequently the gentility of trade cards is only equalled by "prestige" advertising today; though animal dealers are an exception; in the Banks Collection a card advertising some new canary birds has a picture of a perky spotted bird, and G. Pidcock had a robust card describing two "stupendous elephants". The bell is always almost dimly seen in the background, displayed very small with other things which manufacturers of ironwork, smiths, and braziers sold—steel chests, gridirons, and spits. However, "W. Wood, Whitesmith, Pimlico, by His Majesty's letter patent, House Bells, Night Bolts, Water Closets, etc., are hung upon a new construction", has a large bell hanging from a scroll surrounded with locks and bell cranks; and Joseph King, a whitesmith of Bristol, surrounded his picture of jacks and grates with a magnificent rococo border, with a bell hanging from one of its aspiring crockets.

In the next century the increasing use of printed labels and wrapping papers bearing the firm's registered trade-mark, encouraged manufacturers in the use of symbols, and chromo-lithography provided them with the means of dazzling their customers with the richness and intricacy of their devices. The *Trade-marks Journal,* and the Trade Marks filed under class of goods and devices in the Patent Office, show more clearly than anything else the sad decline of the typographer's and trade-mark designer's arts. The richest and most inspiring years are the 1870s; besides bells, there are richly engraved turtles, dark beehives, horses' heads, ravening lions, and striped tigers, and a fat, frightened pussy cat peering through a horse-shoe to become the trade-mark of a wine and spirit merchant. There is hardly any white paper left, every available space has been used to give substance to the principle that it is more pleasurable for the eye to have a complicated and interesting pattern or picture to look at than a piece of arid visual Calvinism. Today, consultant package designers, as they like to be called, have substituted in their art, wire for bones and china tea for blood, and they work on the principle that it is a virtue for the eye to be able to take in the simpering purity of their design and to balance all its subtleties in a few seconds, instead of giving us the rich solidity of the early Bristol tobacco wrappings, or the sumptuous elegance of the Redditch needle packets, or the exquisite world of the cigar-box labels.

But to return to the *Trade-marks Journal.* Before discussing the use of bells as trade-marks, their background must be given by describing others. The cigar-boxes and wine labels are most luxurious visually, with tropical islands and golden vineyards, but more commonplace manufacturers evoke a world equally as moving. The trade-mark of Phospho Guano for instance, which displays a guano-producing bird—auk, gull, or dodo, it is hard to classify it exactly—looks out from a coroneted lunette surrounded by the fruits of the earth and flowers of the field which it helps to grow in such abundance. Old Tom Tobacco has a pussy—more popular for trade-marks than the faithful dog of coloured supplement art—sitting up with a pipe of the fragrant weed in a front paw, while he blows out a puff of smoke. A race for the Champagne Stakes had jockeys riding four-legged magnums; Oedenvoken of Antwerp's candle labels for Bougie de Cordillera and Bougie du Pacifique each had its appropriate landscape; Egyptian Costumes, a label bearing pictures of the Sphinx and pharaohs and round it in hieroglyphic lettering "Bon Bons and Crackers including Surprise Cosaques"; Percy's Mirror Blacking, had an ostler shaving in his reflection in a top-boot; there is Early Bird Tobacco; Brighton Sea Salt, with a hornpipe-dancing tar; and the horrific school which has, for example, a picture of a breast exhauster in use; then there is the fast disappearing convention of the gold medal, appearing on high-class goods such as piano-wire and violin-strings, reproduced in gold and cataloguing the forgotten exhibitions of the nineteenth century.

There is also the litany of names and slogans. Messrs. Bell and Black under their trade-mark of a bell made matches—Patent Vesuvians, Wax Vestas, Fixed Stars, and Camphorated Lights. Copes the tobacco manufacturers dispensed with elaborate designs and relied on the word; they sold tobaccos called Prairie Flower, Peach Blossom, Old Crow, Rose Bud, Queen of the Tropics, Rambler, Sorcerer, Star of the East, and Talisman. Soap also needs a memorable name stamped firmly on it to last till washed away; there were London Pales, Dark Browns, Crown Yellows, and Double Primroses, Gossage's Best Mottled, Fine Pale, Primrose, and Prize Medal Wax Pale.

Bells were popular with musical instrument makers irrespective of their names, perhaps because of the connotation of as clear as a bell, and the religious associations of bells with churches and the consequent implication that music is not only the food of love, but can fortify the soul as well as enflame the passions. But many manufacturers found the bell a good, simple symbol; D. Storer, a manu-

179

facturer of patent medicines, used it; there was Bull and Bell brand paint, a careering bull charged with a bell; and a steel and wire drawer had a bell charged with bell tents. Tobacco, however, seems to provide the manufacturer and the artist with the best inspiration. Messrs. J. and F. Bell naturally used bells most; Ringer's mark is a bell against a brick wall, while Bell's used on their labels three bells either tied together by the canons with a ribbon, or hanging side by side from a bar.

The bells in trade-marks are as silent as the wooden bell which hung in the Chapel of St. Mary Magdalene at Ripon and the dumb-bells and Indian clubs which were flourished before breakfast. One inventor fitted small bells to Indian clubs so that if many people were swinging them round, above and behind their heads, the ringing would keep time and be a substitute for the Blue Danube, always a popular accompaniment for Indian-club displays. All dumb-bells were not silent, and one pair was made to speak when it was fitted with clockwork bells operated by pressing a button so that a gentleman could call his valet while he was exercising.

Other silent bells are the flat canvas representations of the bells of St. Mary le Bow, which wobble to and fro, in the belfry scene, or fairy bell foundry transformation in the pantomime of Dick Whittington. To be born within the sound of the real Bow Bells is the definition of a true Londoner, though now that the city is all offices, there are far fewer people who can claim that distinction today. Richard Whittington is supposed to have heard them ringing,

Turn again Whittington
Lord Mayor of London,

prophesying his successful career. He was not, as one might wish, the child of humble parents, but the son of Sir William Whittington. He became a mercer, and was Lord Mayor in

1397-8, 1406-7, and 1419-20, and his benefactions included a hospital for thirteen poor men, and in his last term of office as Lord Mayor he paid for building the greater part of the new library of the Greyfriars; he died in 1423. The legend of his ill treatment by Fitzwarren's cook, and the purchase of his cat by the King of Barbary for a vast sum first appeared in 1605, as a ballad and a play. The pantomime version of the story is the best one, it disregards all the facts.

The scene in which Dick hears the bells is set on Highgate Hill in high summer, the grass is dazzlingly green and there should be rabbits, large white, and black blotchy ones bundling about under a piece of netting inside a cave cut into the bank on which Dick and Puss eventually fall asleep. The back drop is painted with a panorama of a smokeless London, and a good anachronistic one will have the dome of St. Paul's, which scholars in the audience can poo poo, in the same way that they will explain to their children that the cat is not really a cat at all but a corruption of the French *achat,* or buying and selling at a profit. But nobody else bothers with that. Dick and Puss enter tired after their long walk, the cat making some plaintive miaows, while Dick sympathises with him, then a man in the orchestra starts to play some tubular bells, Bim Bom Pega Bega, Turketyl, and Tatwin. In some productions Dick will immediately interpret the meaning of the bells, but in others he will go to sleep, and then a celestial choir sings, "Turn again Whittington Lord Mayor of London" as the lights fade on the saddest scene in the pantomime; then there may be a transformation to the fairy bell foundry. But whatever happens Dick goes off to North Africa with a pheasant's feather in his hat, and there the promise of the fairy queen that:

No harm shall come to Whittington or his CAT,
That is my steadfast pledge vile RAT,

is fulfilled, for Puss kills the vile rodent, and Dick is able to marry Alice Fitzwarren, and so proceed to a wedding peal.

In a rhetorical but undeniable way bells lead from the rattle to the death-knell with all the experiences of life tied to their sound. The last time that a toy fire-engine was a world, the first cliché thought on the sadness of church bells on a summer evening, dad's death in a belfry disaster; after adolescence the study will broaden out to chorus girls miming ponies, and the nipper ringing the crotals on his harness. From there it all begins again, bringing for every generation its own inventions, nostalgia, and din.

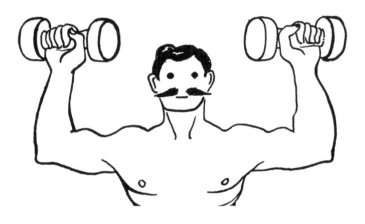

APPENDIX A
IRVING IN *THE BELLS*
by
ROBERT AICKMAN

"The excitement which lies in the words: 'I am going to see Irving in *The Bells*'."

GORDON CRAIG

IN 1869 Emile Erckmann and Louis Gratrien Charles Chatrian, two writers from Lorraine who for literary purposes merged into the joint personality Erckmann-Chatrian, published a play entitled *Le Juif Polonais*. They described it is "une simple étude dramatique tente sans aucune préoccupation du théâtre". But it was a period when there were more working theatres in Europe than ever before (and many more than there are today); and in the same year the play was produced at the Théâtre Cluny. Not for the first time in its history, the English theatre was for original invention largely dependent upon the French; so that within a year or two, at least two English versions of the play were going the rounds of the managers, one, by Sir Francis Burnard, later to become Editor of *Punch,* entitled *Paul Zegers or The Dream of Retribution,* the other, by Leopold Lewis, entitled *The Bells.* Lewis was a solicitor, as his name suggests; but a solicitor of Bohemian habits. He had a large red moustache.

Colonel Hezekiah Linthicum Bateman was a theatrical manager from Baltimore, whose wife, Sidney Cowell, and three daughters, Kate, Isabel, and Virginia, all achieved stage careers of varying degrees of distinction. To launch his second child (who died at an advanced age as an Anglican Mother Superior), Colonel Bateman took a lease of the Lyceum Theatre, London, which had been out of luck for a long time; and engaged to support his daughter a not unknown, but certainly not well-known, actor of thirty-three, named Henry Irving, who had already played more than six hundred parts, mostly out of London.

The venture made a poor start with a version (called *Fanchette*) by Mrs. Bateman of George Sand's *La Petite Fadette*; and the improvement was unremarkable when to *Fanchette* was added a dramatisation of *Pickwick Papers* by James Albery, in which Irving played Jingle. At the time he was engaged, Irving had obtained a promise from Bateman to produce *The Bells*; and after the failure of *Fanchette*, Bateman, in desperation and reduced to taking subsidies, from his prosperous daughter Kate, kept his promise. The result, on Saturday November 25th, 1871, was perhaps the most famous first night in English theatrical history. Certainly only the first appearances of Garrick (as Richard III) at Goodman's Fields Theatre and of Edmund Kean (as Shylock) at Drury Lane can be compared with it.

As in those earlier cases, the house was ill-filled and apathetic: by the end of Irving's performance the last great English actor was an established national figure. The original production enjoyed the then remarkable run of one hundred and fifty-one performances. Irving played *The Bells* before Queen Victoria and the Prince and Princess of Wales at Sandringham; and it was the play with which he opened the first of his astonishing American tours. In the last week of his life, he was to have played it on the Saturday night at the Theatre Royal, Bradford; but, having been persuaded to substitute a piece less physically exacting, died after the performance of Tennyson's *Becket* on the Friday. To have seen Irving in *The Bells* was for a long time the unquestioned fundamental of a British theatrical education; and never to have seen him was to connote oneself, in the widest circles and among all classes, what Shakespeare calls a booby. "*The Bells,*" wrote James Agate, "apart from the first act, which was heartbreaking, was a piffling melodrama. I would rather see the old man in it than any ten of today's young men playing Oedipus, Lear, and the entire classic repertory. In my considered view, great acting in this country died with Irving, and I haven't seen smell or sight or hearing or feel or taste of it since. If our young playgoers saw Irving they would burst like electric-light bulbs."

Like many critics in our unlettered theatre, Agate judged players better than plays; but it is hard to deny that about *The Bells* he was right. Mathias, the innkeeper in an Alsatian village, has waylaid one of his customers, a Polish Jew, and murdered him with a hatchet for the gold in his belt, afterwards throwing the body into a limekiln. On the gold Mathias has prospered, and his daughter is about to marry the chief of police. But all the time Mathias has been haunted by the sound of the Jew's sleigh-bells as he heard them coming across the snow on the night of the murder; and on the eve of the wedding he dreams that he is forced into a confession by a mesmerist whom he has seen the day before at a fair. The play ends with his crying out to his family "Take the rope from my neck", and his death from conscience. In its way it is a promising story; but the dialogue is wooden and the treatment unsubtle. There are some good lines: "How the dogs howl on Daniel's farm!" shudders Mathias on his way to the murder; and the title must be one of the best ever hit upon. But still it is a play which leaves almost everything to the actor.

Mr. Gordon Craig has made a brilliant and detailed analysis of what Irving did with it; and Professor F. S. Boas, a distinguished authority, compares the effect with that made by Macbeth. To the day of his death forty years later, my father could represent Irving's delivery of the line about the dogs; and Irving, lowering his glass in the first act upon the mention of the "Polish Jew's winter", has passed into history, as has his removal from Mathias's daughter's dowry of a piece of the Jew's gold, and subsequent wiping of his hands. Irving's first entrance was another great moment. It is the worst night since the Polish Jew was murdered, and fear and tension are steadily rising among the little group in the ill-lit inn; suddenly Mathias enters through the door at the back, his cloak spattered with snow: "It is I." The physical energy which Irving put into the part must also be stressed; it is remarkably apparent in the excellent extant photographs of his performance. But fundamentally Irving did with Mathias what he did with Shylock; turned an object of vilification, a butt, into an object of sympathy, and enlarged the compassion of entire audiences thereby. In a queer way the creaking piece has symbolism and a prophecy of Freud's explorations into the unconscious; and Irving, contrary to popular belief, was the most progressive of managers (in the rare good sense). It was Irving who first lowered the curtain between acts; and who revolutionised the whole concept of production. (For *The Bells* Hawes Craven, one of the best realistic scene-painters, provided splendid and beautiful, though ultimately somewhat battered, sets.) With Irving the great art of the theatre reached its brief British apogee. I myself saw Sir John Martin Harvey in the part of Mathias, an outstanding actor and one who at all times specialised in suggesting that behind him, just over his shoulder, stood a ghost; and was properly impressed by how much great histrionic gifts could make of such apparently flat material.

From the first Irving insisted that the bells themselves be mounted on a hoop exactly as if on harness; and that the ringer actually move across the back of the stage instead of ringing different tones from the same position, as would be in accord with theatrical custom. The first sound of the phantom sleigh-bells was possibly for many the supreme moment of the play. The whole idea, like the title, was certainly a wonderful *coup-de-théâtre*. Irving's bells were used by Martin Harvey; and were shown at the admirable London Museum Irving Exhibition, which in 1938 commemorated the centenary of his birth. On the twenty-fifth anniversary of the play, Irving was presented with a silver bell, two feet high, designed by Sir Alfred Gilbert, R.A.

According to the money's-worth custom of the day, *The Bells* on its first night was followed by Albery's Pickwick adaptation with Irving's Jingle. After the performance, the shouting, and the ecstasy, there was, of course, a party. There was more and more champagne until it was nearly day. On their way home, Irving quoted to his wife Kean's famous remark on that similar occasion: "Mary! You shall ride in your carriage." But Mrs. Irving cared for neither theatricals nor swelled heads, and asked a simple question: "Are you going on making a fool of yourself like this all your life?" Irving stopped the cab. He got out. He never returned home. He never spoke to his wife again. Mrs. Irving had taken the decisive step which finally assured his career of greatness. (One has only to think of Mrs. Edmund Kean.) It was uncharacteristically apt that she should take this step on the first night of *The Bells*.

Authorities:—
Henry Irving by Laurence Irving (Faber and Faber).
We Saw Him Act edited by H. A. Saintsbury and Cecil Palmer (Hurst and Blackett).
Henry Irving by Edward Gordon Craig (J. M. Dent).
My Father's reminiscences.

APPENDIX B
THE BELLS OF BEALINGS HOUSE
by
ROBERT AICKMAN

They are neither man nor woman—
They are neither brute nor human—
They are Ghouls:
And their king it is who tolls.
EDGAR ALLAN POE

L ORD RAGLAN has shown how little truth there is in history; and has well suggested that few things should be accepted as historical which were not set down in writing at more or less the time of occurrence by a competent observer. Judged by this reasonable test (which, it should be noted, transmutes most of ancient history into myth), the number of authentic supernatural manifestations is surprisingly large. But few are better authenticated than the ringing of the bells at Bealings House in 1834.

Bealings is today well known as one of the few stations beyond Ipswich at which the Yarmouth and Lowestoft main-line trains fail to stop. The station is seven and a quarter miles from Ipswich, and three miles from Woodbridge. There are two villages, Bealings Magna and Bealings Parva. Their combined population can hardly exceed four hundred. Bealings House lies a mile or so to the west of both of them. It is important to note at the outset that the disturbances took place at Bealings *House* and not at Bealings Hall. In his account of the episode, the late Commander Rupert T. Gould, although otherwise as lucid,

188

comprehensive, and witty as he always was (in all three respects he was in a class by himself among writers on the paranormal), curiously omits to mention the exact address; and it would be disastrous if students of the psychic were to make the long journey only to gaze at the wrong (but more readily accessible) mansion. Bealings House was built in the eighteenth century and stands in a small park. The River Finn flows near it, to join the River Deben at Martlesham.

The bells began to ring on Sunday February 2nd, 1834; and in the subsequent fifty-four days there was not one without paranormal ringing, often both protracted and frenzied. It may be stated with confidence that there is no case on record of a paranormal occurrence at once so long and so continuously sustained, and so admirably attested. Major Edward Moor, the owner of the house, was a Fellow of the Royal Society; he perceived from the first the importance of recording the course of events; supplied several detailed bulletins to the *Ipswich Journal* while the ringing was still going on; and ultimately wrote and published *Bealings Bells. An account of the Mysterious Ringing of Bells at Great Bealings, Suffolk, in 1834.* Furthermore, being retired, he had the leisure needed to make a competent thing of the investigation.

The dining-room bell began it while the Major was at church. It rang on three separate occasions. "At this, the servants left in the house, a man and woman, were surprised; no person or cause being perceptible, though sought." On the next day, Monday, the same bell rang three or four times, on the last occasion within the Major's hearing. But it was on the Tuesday that the ringing began in earnest. "I left home early, and returned before five in the afternoon. I was immediately told that 'all the bells in the kitchen had been ringing violently'. A peal at that moment sounded in my ears. I proceeded thither and learned from the cook that the 'five bells on the right' had, since about three o'clock, been frequently so affected. There are nine bells in a row, about a foot apart, ten feet from the floor, and twelve from the fire; not over it. While I was intently looking at the bells, and listening to the relation that the ringings had occurred at intervals of about a quarter of an hour, the same five bells rang violently; so violently was it that I should not have been surprised if they had been shaken from their fastenings." After that the ringings continued, initially at intervals of ten or fifteen minutes, but later at lengthening intervals, until 7.45, "when the last peal of Tuesday sounded". At about 8.45 a single bell, that from an unoccupied attic, sounded gently. From the outset the ringings were also regularly witnessed by Major Moor's son, Edward James Moor, who later became Rector of Great Bealings.

From then until March 27th, when the ringings ceased as suddenly and inexplicably as they had begun, the house might well have been regarded as uninhabitable. (In a lesser case of the same kind, that of No. 9 Earl Street, Westminster, Mr. Harry Price reports that "the ringing was so loud and persistent that it sent one of the maidservants into convulsions"; but Major Moor informs us that, happily, even by the time of the later ringings on the first Tuesday, the cook "had heard and seen so many that she was now unmoved".) The ringings were remarkably consistent; the changes were rung by the five bells heard on the Tuesday, and by three other bells; and when neither the five nor the three were ringing, there were occasional solo pealings by the single bell from the attic and by one other bell, almost as if the ringers were sending messages to or wrangling with one another. Not the least unnerving aspect of the infestation was the extreme violence of the ringings: Major Moor was quite unable to produce ringings of comparable violence either by agitating the bell-handles in the usual way or by dragging on the wires.

The installation was of the type then universal in houses of consequence throughout the country. The actual bells depended from springs in a row in the kitchen; and were operated by wires passing along the walls of the house, and leading to "pulls" in the different rooms. "The wires of the five and of the three pealers," wrote the Major, "are visible in their whole course, from their pulls to the bells, save where they go through walls, in which the holes seem no bigger than is necessary. The wires of the two single bells are also visible, except where they go through floors or walls." There were twelve bells in all; the twelfth, the front-door bell, never participated in the paranormal ringings. All who have known such installations will agree that, if reasonably well maintained, they are remarkably efficient (commonly much more so than their electrical successors); and the Major states that only one of the bell runs, that from the breakfast-room, had needed repair within the previous twenty-eight years.

The Major carried out a number of tests and experiments to account for the ringings and to eliminate all possibility of normal causation. He achieved the latter end, but not the former. Perhaps his most interesting discovery was that even by dragging with a hoe on five bell wires at once, it was possible to produce nothing more than a slight tinkling, and that only by discreet and gentle manipulation. Violent lugging produced no sound at all; an eerie contrast to the dæmonic ringings which shook the house at quarter-hourly intervals while the experiment was in progress. The Major even read a short paper on the ringings to "six or eight very intelligent gentlemen at Woodbridge"; but they could only return him to his noisy abode with such suggestions as that there must be a monkey in the house. "But what matters?" the Major concluded, with slight, entirely comprehensible hysteria. "Neither I, nor the servants, singly or together, nor anyone, be he whom he may, could or can, I aver, work the wonderment that I and more than half a score others saw." He did consider "some hitherto undiscovered law of electricity or galvanism—latent—brought into activity only by certain combinations of metallic alloys, in certain co-extension of parallelisms, straightness or angles"; but his final word on the ringings was: "I will here note, once for all, that after much consideration I cannot reach any procedure by which they have been or can be produced."

The work of Mr. Harry Price and others suggests that in certain circumstances, almost impossible dependably to prearrange, energy, and even conceivably some parts of intelligence, can become disembodied and operate with seeming autonomy. Such is the at present most likely explanation of much that happens at the (rare) authentic séance: such the possible explanation of the "poltergeist disturbance," of which the ringing of the bells at Bealings House provides such a notable example. There are many other less striking but still well-supported cases of such ringings: notably, perhaps, those at Greenwich Hospital and at Borley Rectory, "the most haunted house in England," which stood at no great distance from Bealings. Major Moor himself describes several parallel cases (not all of them satisfactory) in his little book.

There is much evidence that those who live with the supernatural soon cease to fear it; and we have Major Moor's cook as a case in point. Indeed, there seems to survive no record of a single defection from the Major's domestic staff at the time of the ringings. But it is not everyone who could pass untroubled through such a long and clamorous visitation; nor do our poor scraps of psychic science at all suffice finally to rout the idea that such tumults may each be, in the words of Major Moor's friend, Edward Fitzgerald, the slightly cryptic *genius loci* of south-east Suffolk, "A Muezzin from the tower of darkness."

Authorities:—

Bealings Bells. An Account of the Mysterious Ringing of Bells at Great Bealings, Suffolk, in 1834 by Major Edward Moor, F.R.S. (John Loder, Woodbridge, 1841).

Enigmas by Lt.-Commander Rupert T. Gould, R.N. (Ret.) (Geoffrey Bles).

Poltergeist over England by Harry Price (Country Life).

BIBLIOGRAPHY

Allen, F. J.: *The Great Church Towers of England.* 1932.
Andrews, W.: *Curious Church Customs.* 1895.
Austen, G.: *Historical Sermon on York Minster Bells.* 1926.
Banister, W.: *The Art and Science of Change Ringing.* 1879.
Batty, Rev. R. E.: *Church Bells.* 1850.
Beaufoy, Samuel: *The Ringer's True Guide.* 1804.
Beaumont, W.: *Chapter on Bells.* 1888.
Benson, G.: *The Bells of the Ancient Churches of York.* 1885.
Benton, G. M.: *The Bells and Ringing Annals of Saffron Walden.* 1921.
Besant, Sir Walter: *London in the Eighteenth Century.* 1925.
Blair, R.: *Church Bells of Durham.* 1883-90.
— *Church Bells of Northumberland.* 1883-90.
Blakemore, Thomas: See; Jones, William.
Blunt, W.: *The Use and Abuse of Church Bells.* 1846.
Brand, John: *Observations on Popular Antiquities.* 1813.
Briscoe, J. P.: *Curiosities of the Belfry.* 1883.
Brown, A. W.: *The History and Antiquities of Bells.* 1857.
— *The Law of Church Bells.* 1857.
C., Lady H.: *Something About Bells Told to Little Folks.* 1878.
Campanalogia: A Poem in Praise of Ringing, by the author of *The Shrubs of Parnassus* (i.e. William Woty). 1761.
Campanalogia; or the Art of Ringing Improved. 1677. (The dedication is signed F. S., i.e. Fabian Stedman.)
Campanalogia Improved: or the Art of Ringing made Easie (by J. D. and C. M.). 1702.
Cassell's Book of Sports and Pastimes.
Central Council of Church Bell Ringers:
A Glossary of the Technical Terms Employed in Connection with Church Bells. 1901.
A Collection of Peals. 1904-8.
A Collection of Legitimate Methods. 1907.
The Report of a Conference Between the Society for the Protection of Ancient Buildings and the Central Council of Church Bell Ringers. 1922.
Instructions on the Care and Use of Church Bells. 1925.

Instruction Sheets for Ringing Standard Methods. 1930.
A Collection of Triples Methods. 1935.
Variation and Transposition. 1936.
Hints for Instructors and Beginners in the Proper Method of Handling a Bell Rope. 1939.
A Handbook on the Installation, Preservation and Repair of Bells, Bell Frames and Fittings. 1948.
Four Way Table of Minor Methods. 1948.
Change Ringing on Handbells. 1949.
A Collection of Compositions in the Popular Major Methods. 1950.
A Model Code of Rules Suitable for a Society or Company of Ringers. 1950.
A Collection of Plain Major Methods. 1952.
Cescinsky and Webster: *English Domestic Clocks.* 1913.
Cheetham, F. H.: *The Church Bells of Lancashire.* 1915-21.
Clark, J. W.: *King's College Bells.* 1879.
Clarke, J. E. T.: *Musical Boxes.* 1952.
Clouston, R. W. M.: *Church Bells of Renfrewshire and Dumbartonshire.* 1947.
— *Church Bells of Ayrshire.* 1947.
— *Church Bells of Flintshire.* 1951.
— *Scottish Rings of Bells.* 1951.
— *Church Bells of Stirlingshire.* 1952.
Cocks, A. H.: *Church Bells of Buckinghamshire.* 1897.
Colchester, W. E.: *Hampshire Church Bells.* 1920.
Coleman, S. N.: *Bells: their History, Legends, Making and Uses.* 1928.
Cooper, J. E.: *Bellringers and Bellringing.* 1950.
Corrigan, A. J.: *Some Peals of Grandsire Triples.* 1947.
— *160 Unnamed Major Surprise Methods in Place Notation.* 1947.
— *100 Surprise Methods in Place Notation.* 1947.
— *370 Surprise Major Methods.* 1948.
— *350 Surprise Royal and Maximus Methods.* 1949.
— *The Half-Lead System of Extracting False Course Heads in Treble Bob Methods.* 1950.
— *Dates of First Peals and Progressive Lengths in all Published Surprise Methods, on Eight, Ten, or Twelve Bells up to 31 December 1949.* 1950.
Cox, Rev. J. C.: *Notes on the Churches of Derbyshire.* 1875-9.
Cox, Nicholas: *The Gentleman's Recreation.* 1686.
Croome, T. B.: *A Few Words on Bells and Bellringing.* 1851.
Davies, C. D. P.: *Stedman:* (incorporating *The Historic Peals and General History,* by Jasper Whitfield Snowdon.) 1903.
— *Selected and Popular Surprise Methods for Six and Eight Bells* (incorporating *The History of Cambridge.*

Superlative and London Surprise Major, by Jasper Whitfield Snowdon). 1927.
— *The Bellringer.* 1927.
— *Odds and Ends of Grandsire Triples.* 1929.
Dearmer, P.: *Church Bells.* 1908 (with Walters, H. B.).
Deedes, C.: *The Church Bells of Essex.* 1909 (with Walters, H. B.).
Denison, E. Beckett (Baron Grimthorpe): *A Rudimentary Treatise on Clocks, Watches and Bells.* 1903.
Dove, R. H.: *A Bellringer's Guide to the Church Bells of Britain and Ringing Peals of the World.* 1950.
Downman, E. A.: *Ancient Church Bells in England.* 1898.
Dunkin, E. H. W.: *The Church Bells of Cornwall.* 1878.
Earwaker, J. P.: *Church Bells of Cheshire.* (Hundred of Macclesfield) 1877-80.
Eeles, F. C.: *The Church and Other Bells of Kincardineshire.* 1897.
— *The Church Bells of Linlithgowshire.* 1913.
Ellacombe, Rev. H. T.: *The Bells of the Church, a Sermon.* 1862.
— *Sundry Words About Bells* (with W. T. Maunsell and others). 1864.
— *The Church Bells of Devon.* 1867.
— *Practical Remarks on Belfries and Ringers.* 1871.
— *Bells of the Church.* 1872. (A supplement to the *Church Bells of Devon,* with which it is usually bound.)
— *The Bells of Exeter Cathedral.* 1874.
— *The Voice of the Church Bells.* 1875.
— *The Church Bells of Somerset.* 1875.
— *The Church Bells of Gloucestershire.* 1881.
Elliott, M.: *Flowers of Instruction or Familiar Subjects in Verse.* 1820.
Evans, J. T.: *The Church Plate of Radnorshire.* 1910.
— *The Church Plate of Breconshire.* 1912.
Fidler, J. P.: *Method Splicing.* 1925.
Fletcher, C. W.: *Handbell Ringing.* 1888.
Flitton, A. R.: *The Bells of Trumpington, Cambridgeshire.* 1926.
Fosbroke, T. D.: *Encyclopedia of Antiquities.* 1840.
Freeman, G. E.: *Practical Falconry.* 1869.
Gatty, Dr. A.: *The Bell, its Origin, History and Uses.* 1847.
Gillett and Johnston, Ltd.: *Church Bells, Carillons, Tower Clocks, Electric Clocks.* 1939.
Goldsmith, J. S.: *A Great Adventure.* 1935.
Goslin, S. B.: *First Steps in Bellringing.* 1877.
— *The ABC of Musical Handbell Ringing.* 1879.
— *The Musical Handbell Ringer's Instructor.* 1891.

Graham, W.: *Brassfounder's Manual*. 1868.

Green, E. T.: *Towers and Spires, their Design and Arrangement*. 1908.

"Guardian": *Church Bells and Bellringing*. 1907.

Harrison, J.: *Introduction to a Treatise on the Proportion, etc., of Bells*. 1831.

Harrison, R.: *Bells of the Isle*. 1943.

Heal, Sir Ambrose: *London Tradesmen's Cards of the Eighteenth Century*. 1925.

Hewitt and Rhodes: *Instructions for Electric Car Drivers and Conductors*. 1902.

Heywood, Sir A. P.: *A Treatise on Duffield*. 1888.

— *Bell Towers and Bell Hanging*. 1914.

Hill, A. D.: *The Church Bells of Winchester*. 1877.

Hole, Christina: *English Custom and Usage*. 1941.

— *English Home Life, 1500-1800*. 1947.

— *English Sports and Pastimes*. 1949.

Hone, W.: *Everyday Book*. 1831.

- - *Year Book*. 1832.

Hope, R. C.: *English Bell Founders*. 1893.

Howes, R.: *Village Bells*. 1947.

Howgrave-Graham, R. P.: "Some Clocks and Jacks", *Archæologia*, LXXVII. 1928.

Hoyle, E.: *The History of Barnsley Old Church*. 1891.

Hubbard, H.: *Elements of Campanalogia*. 1845.

Husbandman's Magazine. 1684.

Jones, William: with Blakemore, Thomas: and Reeves, J.: *Clavis Campanalogia, or a Key to the Art of Ringing*. 1788.

Kelsall, C.: *A Letter on Bells*. 1836.

Lambert's *Countryman's Treasure*.

Lancashire Association of Change Ringers: *Rules and Diagrams for the Instruction of Beginners*. 1937.

Larwood and Hotten: *English Inn Signs*. 1951.

L'Estrange, J.: *The Church Bells of Norfolk*. 1874.

Lewty, H. A.: *Church Bells*. 1932.

Lomax, B.: *Bells and Bell-ringers*. 1879.

Lukis, W. C.: *An Account of Church Bells, with Some Notices of Wiltshire Bells and Bell Founders*. 1857.

— *Have You Ever Seen the Bells of Your Church?* 1858.

— *How Many Bells Are There, And Are They in Good Order?* 1858.

Lynam, C.: *The Church Bells of Staffordshire*. 1887.

M., C.: See *Campanalogia Improved*.

Mackie, S. J.: *Great Paul*. 1882.

Madge, S. J.: *Moulton Church and Its Bells*. 1895.

Maunsell, W. T.: *Church Bells and Ringing*. 1861.

Maunsell, W. T.: *Sundry Words About Bells* (with H. T. Ellacombe). 1864.

Meneely, E. A., and G. R.: *Church, Academy, Factory, and Other Bells.* 1871.

Moor, E.: *Bealings Bells, an Account of the Mysterious Ringing of Bells at Great Bealings, Suffolk.* 1841.

Morris, Ernest: *The History and Art of Change Ringing.* 1931.

— "Tintinnabula", *Apollo*, September 1934.

— "Ships' Bells", *Blue Peter*, October 1934.

— *Legends o' the Bells.* 1935.

— "Substitutes for Bells", *City Chimes*, August 1936.

— "Ancient Bells of Celtic Saints", *Apollo*, December 1938.

— *Bells of all Nations.* 1951.

— "Chronology of British Bellfounders," *Musical Year Book*, Vol VI, 1949-50.

— "Musical Aspects of Bellringing", *Musical Year Book*, Vol. VII, 1951-2.

Morrison, Gouvernour: *Bells—History and Romance.* 1932.

Myers, T. H.: *Bells and Bell Lore.* 1916.

Nares, R.: *A Glossary.* 1822.

Nichols, J. R.: *Bells thro' the Ages.* 1928.

North, T.: *The Church Bells of Leicestershire.* 1876.

— *The Church Bells of Northamptonshire.* 1878.

— *The Church Bells of Rutland.* 1880.

— *The Church Bells of Lincolnshire.* 1882.

— *The Church Bells of Bedfordshire.* 1883.

— *The Church Bells of Hertfordshire.* 1886.

— *English Bells and Bell Lore.* 1888.

Owen, T. M. N.: *The Church Bells of Huntingdonshire.* 1899.

Park, G. R.: *The Church Bells of Holderness.* 1898.

Pearson, C.: *Church Bells of Devon.* 1888.

Pearson, W. C.: *Some Particulars of the Principal Rings of Bells in the Eastern Counties.* 1910.

Perkins, J. H. T.: *The Organ and Bells of Westminster Abbey.* 1937.

Poppleton, J. E.: *Church Bells of Yorkshire—West Riding.* 1902.

Powell, E. S.: *Inventory of the Church Bells of Northamptonshire and Rutland in 1938.* 1938.

— and M.: *The Ringer's Handbook.* 1946.

Powell, J. P.: *Touches of Stedman's Triples.* 1828.

Price, F. P.: *The Carillon.* 1933.

Raven, J. J.: *Church Bells of Cambridgeshire.* 1869.

— *Church Bells of Suffolk.* 1890.

— *The Church Bells of Dorset.* 1903-6.

— *The Bells of England.* 1906.

Reeves, J.: See Jones, William.

Rice, W. G.: *Carillon Music and Singing Towers of the Old and New World.* 1930.

Rigby, F. F.: *Elementary Change Ringing.* 1946.

Robinson, Rev. F. E.: *Among the Bells.* 1909.

Rock, D.: *Church of Our Fathers, 1903-5.*

Roe, J., and Broome, M.: *Plain Bob and Grandsire Methods.* 1950.

Roslyn, H. E.: *The History of the Ancient Society of St. Stephen's Ringers, Bristol.* 1928.

Rudhall, A.: *A Catalogue of Peals of Bells and of Bells in, and for Peals, cast since 1664, by A. R. of Gloucester.* 1715.

Saunders, W. J.: *Electric Bells.* 1927.

Sayers, Dorothy L.: *The Nine Tailors.* 1934.

Scholefield, D.: *A Supplement to the Clavis.* 1853.

Sharpe, F.: *The Church Bells of Radnorshire.* 1946.
— *The Church Bells of Oxfordshire.* 1949-53.
— *The Church Bells of Berkshire.* 1940.

Shepherd, E. C.: *Double Norwich Court Bob Caters.* 1947.
— *The Tower and Bells of Solihull Church.* 1952.
— *St. Martin's Youths.* 1953.

Shipway, W.: *The Campanalogia: or Universal Instructor in the Art of Ringing.* 1816.

Simpson, A. B.: *Why Bells Sound out of Tune.* 1897.

Smith, J. T.: *English Guilds.* 1924.

Snowdon, Jasper W.: *A Treatise on Treble Bob.* 1878.
— *Standard Methods in the Art of Change Ringing.* 1881.
— *Grandsire, the Method its Peals and History.* 1888.
— *Collection of Historical Peals—the History of Stedman's Principle.* 1903. See Davies, C. D. P.
— *History of Cambridge, Superlative, and London Surprise Major.* 1927. See Davies, C. D. P.
— *Ropesight.* 1880.

Sottanstall, W.: *Elements of Campanalogia.* 1867.

Stahlschmidt, J. C. L.: *Surrey Bells and London Bellfounders.* 1884.
— *The Church Bells of Kent.* 1887.

Stedman, Fabian: See *Campanalogia* and *Tintinnalogia.*

Stow, John: *Survey of London.* 1908.

Sturmey, Henry: *The Complete Guide to Bicycling.* 1880.
— *The Tricyclist's Indispensable Annual and Handbook.* 1885.
— *On an Autocar through the Length and Breadth of the Land.* 1899.

Taylor, John (the Water Poet): *All the Workes of John Taylor the Water Poet.* 1630.

Taylor, John, and Company: *The Carillon*. 1927.
Thackrah, B.: *The Art of Change Ringing*. 1852.
Thompson, W. H.: *A Note on Grandsire Triples*. 1886.
— *Diagram of a System of Peals of Union Triples*. 1893.
Thurlow, A. G. G.: *The Church Bells and Ringers of Norwich*. 1947.
Tilley, H. T.: *The Church Bells of Warwickshire*. 1910 (with Walters, H. B.).
Tintinnalogia: or the Art of Ringing. Printed by W. G. for Fabian Stedman. 1668.
Trollope, J. Armiger: *Collection of Triples Methods*. 1935.
— *The College Youths: a History of the Society*. 1937.
— *Stedman*. 1938.
Troyte, C. A. W.: *Change Ringing*. 1869.
Troyte, J. E. A. and R. H. D. A.: *Change Ringers Guide to the Steeples of England*. 1879.
Turner, J. M.: *The Art and Science of Handbell Ringing*. 1950.
Tyack, G. S.: *A Book About Bells*. 1898.
Tyssen, A. D.: *The Church Bells of Sussex*. 1915.
Varah, W. O.: *Barton-on-Humber Bells*. 1948.
Vesey, N. A.: *Church Bells and the Art of Ringing*. 1950.
Walters, F. W.: *The Romance of Church Bells*. 1938.
Walters, H. B.: *The Church Bells of Worcestershire*. 1901.
— *The Church Bells of Shropshire*. 1902-11.
— *Some Notes on Worcestershire Bell Founders*. 1906.
— *London Church Bells and Bell Founders*. 1907.
— *Church Bells*. 1908 with Dearmer, P.
— *The Church Bells of Essex*. 1909 with Deedes, C.
— *The Church Bells of Warwickshire*. 1910 with Tilley, H. T.
— *The Gloucestershire Bell Foundries*. 1912.
— *Church Bells of England*. 1912.
— *The Church Bells of Somerset*. 1920.
— *Miscellaneous Notes on Gloucestershire Bells*. 1921.
— *The Church Bells of Worcestershire*. 1925-30.
— *Some Thirteenth-century English Bells*. 1926.
— *A Dated Medieval Bell from Minchinhampton*. 1926.
— *The Church Bells of Wiltshire*. 1927-9.
— *Church Bells*. 1937.
White, John: *A Rich Cabinet with Variety of Inventions*. 1677.
Whitehead, Rev. H.: *Church Bells of Cumberland*. 1883-97.
Wickes, C.: *The Spires and Towers of the Medieval Churches of England*. 1859.
Wigram, W.: *Change Ringing Disentangled*. 1880.
Wilkinson, Canon R. F.: *Church Bells of Nottinghamshire*. 1930.

Wood, E. J.: *Curiosities of Clocks and Watches.* 1866.
Wright, A.: *The Church Bells of Monmouthshire.* 1942.
Young, E. A.: *Bell Tones and How to Observe Them.* 1928.
— *English Bells and Their Tuning.* 1928.
PERIODICALS
Church Bells. New Year's Eve, 1871- August 25th, 1906.
Bell News and Ringers' Record. February 1881-December 25th, 1915.
Ringing World. March 24th, 1911 (in progress).
The Ecclesiologist. November 1841-December 1868.

ADDENDA

Bevis, T.A.: *Church Bells of the Fens.* 1957.
— *The Ipswich Bellfounders.* 1966.
Boy Scouts Association: *Bellringer and Senior Bellringer.* 1960.
Camp, J.: *Discovering Bells and Bellringing.* 1968.
Chant, H.: *Method Splicing.* 1966.
Christophers, R. J.: *The Bell Tower of Chichester Cathedral.* 1965.
Cleaver, A.: *The Theory of Change Ringing.* 1965.
Fletcher, H. J.: *The First Book of Bells.* 1965.
Girl Guides Association: *Bellringer.* 1953.
Hilton, J. A.: *Joseph Hatch: The Ulcombe Bellfounder.* 1965.
Legg, M. A.: *A Short History of the Bells of Cranbrook Church.* 1965.
Morris, E.: *Towers and Bells of Britain.* 1955.
— *Tintinnabula.* 1959.
Putterill, J.: *The Church Bells of Thaxted.* 1964.
Sharpe, F.: *The Church Bells of Guernsey.* 1964.
Shepherd, E. C.: *The Sound of Bells.* 1964.
Thompson, G. B.: *A Guide Book to Composition.* 1965.
Tufts, N. P.: *The Art of Handbell Ringing.* 1962.
Watson, D.: *The Handbell Choir.* 1959.
Wilson, W. G.: *On Conducting.* 1954.
— *Change Ringing.* 1965.
York-Bramble, A. E. C.: *The Ringer's Manual of Reference.* 1967.
Periodical
Bells and Bellringing. 1966 (in progress).

Index

Advent, ringing for, 81
Aldbourne, 20
Angelus, 82
Arundel, Thomas of, 27
Aylesbury, 35

Banns peal, 76
Barry, Sir Charles, 152
Basingstoke, 82
Bath, 22, 87
Bauderick, described, 110, 111
Bearnán Cuileáin, 4
Beccles, 165
Beckingham, 76
Bede, the Venerable, 5
Bell, bicycle, 126–130
  Blessed, 3
  of Blood, 3
  Book and Candle, 76
  Boon Day, 86
  Columbian Liberty, 113
  of Conall Cael, 4
  Dagtale, 75, 76
  Ding Dong, 167
  electric, 143–147
  estate, 134
  factory, 134
  founders, accounts of, 111, 112
    medieval, 14, 15, 16, 17
    rivalry of, 23, 24
    present day, 116
  founding, described, 95–107, 113,
    114, 115
  foundry, described, 95, 96
  frame, manufacture of, 109
  Fritter, 89
  Gleaning, 86
  Guttit, 89
  hanging of, 109–111
  Harvest Home, 86
  inn sign, 177
  Lutine, 148
  Market, 85
  Morning, 83, 84, 134
  Mote or Common, 84
  mould, description of, 96
    manufacture of, 96–103
  Oven, 85
  Pan Burn, 89
  passing, 77
  phrases, 172
  Pie, 85
  proverbs, 172, 173
  Pudding, 85
  rhymes, 89, 168, 169
  ropes, manufacture of, 117
  Sacrament, 76
  St. Cuana's, 5
  St. Fillan's, 2
  St. Mura's, 3

Bell of St. Patrick's Will, 2
  Sanctus, 75
  Sebastopol, 93
  Sermon, 76
  Soul, 77
  Tantony, 76
  trade marks, 177–180
  waste, 113
Bell-bastard, 173
Bell-comb, 173
Belles-lettres, 165
Bell-hangers, 109
Bell-horse, 173
Bell-moth, 174
Bell-rope, 174
Bell, Messrs. J. and F., 180
Bellman, 134–136
Bell News, 63, 66
Bell News and Ringing Record, 63
Bells, architecture for, 122–125
  Bealings, 188–192
  Bow, 180, 181
  for burglar alarms, 145
  Canterbury, 17, 174
  casting of, 104–108
  for catching birds, 141
  for cats, 138
  for clocks, 148, 150–155
  Church, control of, 37
    dedication of, 11–12
    destruction of, 17
    earliest, 11
    first dated, 11
    hanging of medieval, 6
  for cows, 132
  dumb, 61, 180
  for ferries, 134
  for fire engines, 131–132
  for games, 171
  glass, 162
  for hawks, 139, 140
  in heraldry, 176
  for horses, 132–134
  for Indian Clubs, 180
  for jokes, 170
  Judas, 82
  for motor cars, 130
  musical instruments, 162
  names for different numbers, 53
  in poetry, 166–169
  as prizes for horse races, 171, 172
  raising of, 8–10
  ring of, defined, x
  'Set' defined, 10
  for starting coaches, 134
  table, 136, 137
  'Bells, The', 183–187
Bells on Trade Cards, 177
  tram, 131
  train, 145–147

Bells, tuning, 108, 109
for watches, 149, 150
ways of ringing, 6–10
wheels of, 5
Berwick on Tweed, 124
Bethnal Green, 156–159
Beverley, 84
Big Ben, 153–155
Birchington, 65
Birmingham, 135
Bishop's Morchard, 19
Bishop's Nympton, 72
Bitterley, 16
Blandifer, Jack, 161
Boston, 124
Brass Bands, 175, 176
Bride's Peal, 77
Bridgwater, 24, 112
Bristol, 29, 36, 83
Brokenborough, 5
Brookland, 122
Builder, The, 158
Burdett Coutts, Baroness, 155–159
Burnard, Sir Francis, 183
Burton Lazars, 122

Call Change competitions, 68–72
ringing, 66–73
Cambridge Camden Society, 38
Cambridge Minor, 57, 58
Campanologia, 49, 51, 55
Campanologists, 13, 14
Campana Mutaphone, 162
Canterbury, 6, 17
Carillons, 161, 162
Caroline, Queen, trial of, 35–37
Carter, Henry, 162
Caters, defined, 53
Caversfield, 11
Change ringing, 48–60
Cross Changes, 50, 51
Cross Peals, names of, 52
definition of, 52, 53
influence on number of bells, 23
invention of, 23
Method, 54, 55
Method defined, 51
Plain Changes, 50, 51
Chatham Dockyard, 134
Chawleigh, 72
Cheapside, 83
Cherubim Minor, 162
Chester, 171
Chesterfield, 37
Chichester, 123, 124
Chiming, defined, 7
Christchurch, Oxford, 18, 20, 84
Christmas ringing, 81
Church Bell Ringers, Central Council
of, 53, 55, 63, 66, 115, 121
Cinques defined, 53
Cire perdue, 114
Clappers, fitting to bell, 109, 111
Claughton, 11
Clocking, defined, 6

Clock Jacks, 160, 161
Clog Beannuighthe, 3
na Fola, 3
Oir, 3
Udhachta Phadraig, 2
College Youths, Ancient Society of,
33, 60, 61, 63, 93
Columbia Market, 157–161
Colyton, 114, 115
Confirmation peal, 77
Congleton, 139
Cope, defined, 96
manufacture of, 99–101, 102
Core, defined, 96
manufacture of, 98–99, 102
Coronation decorations, 93–94
ringing, 92, 94
Corr, William, 19
Cottingham, 82
Cromwell, Thomas, 17
Crotals, 126
Crowcombe, 151
Croyland Abbey, 6
Crystal Palace, 66, 147
Curfew, 83, 84, 134
Cyclist, The, 129

Darbishire, Henry Ashley, 158
Darlington, 36
Daventry, 89
Dawlish, 58
Death Knell, 77, 85
Dekker, Thomas, 135
Denison, Edmund Beckett, Lord
Grimthorpe, 153–155
Devil's Knell, 81
Devon Association of Ringers, 68,
69, 72
Dewsbury, 81
Donne, John, 165, 166
Doubles defined, 53
Down St. Mary, 69, 72
Dubbleday, Margery, 83

East Bergholt, 122
Ecclesfield, 12
Ecclesiological Society, 38
Ecclesiologist, The, 38, 39, 41
Ellacombe, Rev. H. T., 38, 39, 40,
41
Elstow, 124
Elstree, 151
Erith, 54
Executions, ringing for, 78–81
Exeter, 28, 136
Exmouth, 59

Fairford, 175
Faringdon, 36
Feast, Bean, 31, 32
Fire Call, The, 131
Firing, defined, 10
Frodsham, 76
Fuller, Mad Jack, 22
Furnace, described, 103

INDEX

Gargate, Hugh, 11
Gatty, Dr. Alfred, 12
Gauge, described, 96
Gillett and Johnston, 64, 116
Glastonbury, 24, 118
Glastonbury Abbey, 122
Gloucester Cathedral, hour bell, 11
Goldington, 85
Good Friday ringing, 82
Gotches, 164, 165
Grandison, Bishop, 122
Great St. Mary's, Cambridge, 75
Great Tom of Christchurch, 18, 20, 84
Great Tom of Westminster, 152
Guy Fawke's Day, 88
Gwynne, William, 20

Halberton, 68, 72
Halifax, 124
Halstow at Hoo, 55
Hammersmith, 84
Handbells, Irish, 2-5
  Scots, 2
  Welsh, 1
Harlington, 88
Headstock, described, 108
  fitted to bell, 110, 115
Hertford, 36
Hertford, Marquess of, 161
Highgate, 156, 181
Hittisleigh, 168
Holly Village, 156, 157
Holy Cross, Guild of, 135
Holy Trinity, Guild of, 135
Hunting, defined, 50, 51

Imperial Institute, 87
Ingelow, Jean, 172
Inscriptions, English, 20, 21, 22, 23, 24, 25, 83, 86, 89, 153, 154
  Latin, 11, 16, 17, 18, 19
  lettering of, 14, 15, 19, 20
  Medieval, 14, 15, 16, 17
  Norman French, 17
  plaster casts of, x
  rubbings of, 13
  stamped in cope, 101
  for tenor, 21
  for weddings, 22

Kent County Association, 54
Kettering, 169
Kidderminster, 84
Killin, 2
Kings Somborne, 122
Kirby Lonsdale, 173
Knole, 61

Lamerie, Paul, 138
Lancaster, 135
Lee, Samuel, 62
Leeds, Kent, 57
Leitrim, 5
Lent, ringing, 82
Liberal, Kansas, 90
Lincoln's Inn, 84

Liverpool, 64
Llanfechell, Anglesea, 123
Lloyds, 148
Low Belling, 141
Lymington, 36

Magdalen Tower, Oxford, 140
Maidstone, 89
Major, defined, 53
Margate, 65
Marsham, 78
Marston Moretaine, 6, 115, 124
Mary Queen of Scots, 149
Maximus, defined, 53
May day, ringing, 88
May Morning, 140
Maypoles, 88
Mear's Foundry, Whitechapel, 22, 154
Melton Mowbray, 85
Minor, defined, 53
Monarch, ringing for death of, 93
Morris Dancers, 139, 140
Mortehoe, 37, 72
Mott, Robert, 111

Nashe, Thomas, 87
New Brighton, 64
New Year's Eve, ringing, 82
New York, 162, 166
Newcastle upon Tyne, 88
Newgate, 78
Newport, I.O.W., 36
North Devon Six Bell Competition, 68, 72
Northam, 25
Northamptonshire, 89
Norton, Stephen, 14, 15
Norwich, 11, 55, 56, 62, 164

Olney, pancake race, 89-92
Oranges and Lemons, 167
Osney Abbey, 18
Ottery St. Mary, 122
Oxford, clocks in, 151
Oxford Movement, 37

Palmer, Richard, 60, 83
Peal attempt, 57-60
  boards, 55, 56
  defined, 54
  raising in, 45, 46
  kinds of, 57
Penzance, 41
Permutations, 49, 50
Peterborough, 77
Pizzie, Joseph, 20
Powderham, 57
Pyke, T., 24

Quex Tower, 65

Rackenford, 69, 72
Radipole, 122
Reading, 7
Rewe, 69, 72

Ringers, ecclesiastical, 27
 inn name, 177
 jugs, 164, 165
 memorials, 62
 organisation into Guilds, 41
  Societies, 29
 outings, 64–66
 present day, 42–44
 reformation of, 38–42
 rules, 30, 31, 33, 34, 35
 societies, 60–62
 of Westminster, 27
Ringing backwards, defined, 87
 for Canonical Hours, 27
 Changes, see Change Ringing
 defined, 7
 description of, 46–48
 disasters, 47–48
 rounds, 23, 48
Ringing World, The, 61, 63, 66
Ripon, 180
Romsey, 132
Ropesight, defined, 55
Rose Ash, 72
Royal Cumberland Youths, Society
 of, 33, 61, 63, 65
Royal, defined, 53
Rye, 161

St. Anthony, 76
St. Clement Danes, 168
St. Clement's, Eastcheap, 168
St. Dunstan's, Fleet Street, 161
St. Giles, in the Wood, 69, 71, 72
St. Helen's, Worcester, 85
St. Katherine, Guild of, 28
St. Leonard's, Shoreditch, 135
St. Mary le Bow, 180–182
St. Mary Magdalene, 180
St. Patrick, 2, 3, 4
St. Paul's Cathedral, 82, 152
 hour bell, 92
St. Peter ad Vincula, 139
St. Peter's, Nottingham, 83
St. Peter's Society, Sheffield, 64
St. Sepulchre's, 79, 80
St. Stephen's Ringers of Bristol,
 Society of, 29–32
St. Thomas' Day, 81
Salisbury, 118, 123
Sally, defined, x
Sancti Tomaes, 17
Satterleigh, 8
Saundby, 76
Scotter, 33
Selbourne, 12
Shaftesbury, 108
Sherborne, 37
Sherborne Abbey, 86
Shipway, W., 55
Shrewsbury, 62
Shrove Tuesday ringing, 89
Spurring Peal, 76
Stamford, 28, 84
Stedman, Fabian, 49, 50, 51, 55

Stowe, 35
Stratford, 36
Strouton, 76
Sturye, Alice, 17
Swansea, 164
Swimbridge, 72

Tailors, Guild of, 28
Tailors, Nine, 78
Taylor Bell Foundry, 114, 116
Taylor, The Water Poet, 89, 170
Teignmouth, 58
Thieves' School, 139
Thurnby, 37
Ting Tang, 75, 76
Tinnitus Aurium, 165
Tintinnalogia, 49, 115
Tisbury, 19
Tocsin, 86
Tolling, defined, 7
Torquay, 59
Totnes, 84
Treswell, 76
Triples, defined, 53
Twyford, Hants, 87
Tyburn, 81

Victory, H.M.S., 147

Walmsley, 21
Walpole St. Peter, 118
Walsham le Willows, 54
Ware, 169
Warner, John, 153
Welbeck Abbey, 144
Wells Cathedral, 160, 161
Wells, Robert, 21
West Down, 72
Westminster, 123, 155
Westminster Abbey, 93, 151
Westminster, Palace of, 152–154
Wheel, half, 8
 quarter, 8
 whole, 8
 fitted to headstock, 110
 influence of, 10
 on change ringing, 13
 shape of bells, 18
 manufacture, 117
Whitchurch Canonicorum, 88
White, Gilbert, 12
Whitechapel Foundry, 111, 116
Whittington, Dick, 180–182
Winchester, 132
Windsor Castle, 93, 152
Wingrave, 87
Witham on the Hill, 89
Woburn Sands, 124
Wokingham, 83
Wolverhampton, 36
Worcester, 83
World's Columbian Exposition, 112
Wragby, 81

York Minster, 114